Deep Light

Books By Rebecca McClanahan

For Peg —

May There always be

Deep Light

in The darkest places.

New and Selected Poems, 1987-2007

Rebecca McClanahan

Santa Barbara
October 8, 2010

Iris Press
Oak Ridge, Tennessee

Iris Press in an imprint of the Iris Publishing Group, Inc.

www.irisbooks.com

Cover photo from *The Third I (Eye)*
Copyright © 2006 by Whirlwind Creative, Inc.
Photography by Terry Parke
Cover Design by Donald Devet
Typeset by Robert B. Cumming, Jr.

Library of Congress Cataloging-in-Publication Data

McClanahan, Rebecca.
Deep light : new and selected poems, 1987-2007 / Rebecca McClanahan.
   p. cm.
Includes index.
ISBN-13: 978-0-916078-98-0 (hardcover : alk. paper)
ISBN-13: 978-0-916078-99-7 (pbk. : alk. paper)
I. Title.
PS3554.E9274D44 2007
811'.54—dc22

2006024126

ACKNOWLEDGMENTS

Poems herein have been selected from *Naked as Eve* (Copper Beech Press, 2000), *The Intersection of X and Y* (Copper Beech Press, 1996), *One Word Deep* (Ashland Poetry Press, 1993), *Mrs. Houdini* (University Press of Florida, 1989), and *Mother Tongue* (University Press of Florida, 1987). I also wish to thank the editors of the following publications, in which many of the new and selected poems first appeared or were reprinted:

The Best American Poetry 1998 (Scribner), Are You Experienced? Baby Boom Poets at Midlife (University of Iowa Press), The Arts Journal, Bellingham Review, Boomer Girls: American Women Poets Come of Age (University of Iowa Press), Boulevard, Cardinal: A Contemporary Anthology of North Carolina Writers (Jacar Press), Carolina Literary Companion, Carolina Quarterly, Crab Orchard Review, Crescent Review, The Charlotte Observer, The Cortland Review, Crazyhorse, The Crucible, Davidson Miscellany, The Denny Poems, The Devil's Millhopper, Emrys Journal, The Georgia Review, The Gettysburg Review, Global City Review, G. W. Review, Indiana Review, The Kenyon Review, The Laurel Review, Louisville Review, The Lyricist, Malahat Review, Negative Capability, Nimrod, North Carolina Literary Review, A More Perfect Union (St. Martin's), New Virginia Review, No Hiding Place (Down Home Press), O Taste and See (Bottom Dog Press), Orpheus and Company: Contemporary Poems on Greek Mythology (University Press of New England), Painted Bride Quarterly, Pembroke Magazine, Poetry, Proposing on the Brooklyn Bridge (Poetworks/Grayson Books), Quarterly West, Shenandoah, Southern Poetry Review, The Southern Review, St. Andrews Review, Tar River Poetry, Weymouth: An Anthology of Poetry (St. Andrews Press), We Used to be Wives (Fithian Press), and *Wilmington Review.*

I am grateful to many people and institutions for their contribution to my ongoing journey as poet and writer. To my early teachers—A. R. Ammons, Audre Lorde, and George Garrett. To the editors who have supported my work through the years, especially R. T. Smith, David Lynn, Stephen Corey, Peter Stitt, and Dave Smith. To the MacDowell Colony, the New York Foundation for the Arts, the North Carolina Arts Council and Ashland University for fellowships and residencies during the years many of these poems were written. To my students and colleagues in the Queens University MFA program, the Hudson Valley Writers' Center, The Kenyon Review Writers Workshop, and Wildacres Writers Workshop. To my constant and long-loved poet friends Gail Peck and Cathy Smith Bowers. To members of my extended family, both living and dead, for their generosity in trusting me with their stories, their brightest joys and sharpest sorrows. And most especially to Donald Devet, my husband of thirty years, whose humor, intelligence, and energy sustain me, and whose love is my deepest light.

for my nieces and nephews

Ron, Wes, Joy, Jamy, Paul Justyn, Shea,
Paul Vincent, Sarah, Andrew, Jeremy,
Haley, Hanah, Jesse, Michael, Patrick

Contents

I First Light

II Ghost, Kiss

III   Sun, Moon, Star, Pearl

IV   The Angle of Shadow, the Angle of Light

V   Deep Light

I

FIRST LIGHT

...In this light
You are not where you were but you have not moved.

—Alberto Rios,
"A Physics of Sudden Light"

WATCHING MY PARENTS SLEEPING
BESIDE AN OPEN WINDOW NEAR THE SEA

Needing them still, I come
when I can, this time to the sea
where we share a room: their double bed,
my single. Morning fog paints the pale
scene even paler. Lace curtains breathing,
the chenille spread folded back,
my father's feet white sails furled
at the edge of blue pajamas.
Every child's dream, a parent
in each hand, though this child is fifty.
Their bodies fit easily, with room
to spare. When did they grow
so small? *Grow* so small—
as if it were possible to swell
backwards into an earlier self.
On the bureau, their toys
and trinkets. His shaving brush
and pink heart pills, her gardenia
sachet. The tiny spindle that pricks
the daily bubble of blood, her sweet
chemistry. Above our heads
a smoke alarm pulses, its red eye beating.
One more year, I ask the silence.
Last night to launch myself
into sleep I counted their breaths, the tidal
rise and fall I now put my ear to,
the coiled shell of their lives.

The Life I Will Be Born Into

My father is feeding the wood stove its breakfast
of poplar and oak, rousing the drowsy cinders.
My sister and brother are asleep in feather beds,
the warming bricks at their feet now cold
as the headstone one baby sister sleeps beneath.
They are too young to understand where she has gone
or to notice the possibility under their mother's gown.
I hiccup and make my first fist. Mother is a heartbeat
and warm waters rolling over the life I will become,
a child so hungry for stories I will rob
even this moment, this morning that is their lives.
The well is dry, the field a stubble of blunted crops,
but my mother trusts what morning will offer,
latches rubber waders at her thighs and throws
a fishing basket over her shoulder. A cane pole
is her walking stick. The path to Wildcat is ragged
and steep and she weaves between oak roots
that years later will trip me. I ride the waters
of her strength and toss my first tale from the future
into her past: the woman in the creek
is younger than the mother I will remember.
Her hips are wide, the boots planted decisively
on the creek bed. Ripples of water, learning
the borders of her body, thread their way around her.

Now the basket is alive with trout and she hauls
herself into the clearing, water rushing from the pockets
of her trousers: she has gone deeper than she had planned.
She pushes through a tangle of vine, begins the long
climb up the hill, her breath coming in quick hard pants,
a labor punctuated by the whoosh of the pole

brushing against leaves. Had there been an easier path,
she might have taken it. At the house she unloads herself
onto the back steps, empties the waders and squeezes
from her trousers the last drops of Wildcat Creek.
The white paint on the farmhouse is peeling, the porch
mud-speckled from the snouts of piglets that soon
will escape and slurp the poison meant for the fox
who has been slashing the chickens' bellies. But for now
there is this offering and the new sun approves,
sprinkles bits of light through her black hair,
across the flannel jacket. The first trout floats
from the bucket to her hand and she slits it
with a kitchen knife, tossing the entrails to the pink sow
rooting nearby. Within minutes my brother and sister,
eyes still crusted with sleep, will warm their hands
at the wood stove, and my mother will dust the trout
with flour and drop it deep into crackling grease.

Yes

Myrrh is not a gift for the living,
so why these burial beads
my mother sends, thinking of me?
The night I was planted in her,
the dirt was fresh on my sister's grave.
Her name was Sylvia. I have seen the gravestone
nudging its head through the Illinois field
toward an immensity of sky. Sky
is all she recalls of that day, sky
and plow horses through the gray snow
and how No was the only word she could form:
No to her children and No to her husband
and No to her own next day. How it crept in,
she cannot remember, but next summer
she sat in church in a black crepe
maternity dress and said Yes to something
and light sneaked through her white gloves
and beneath her hat and she named me Rebecca,
from the Bible, a month before I was born

and August loped in, heavy and hot
as their Irish setter with the one glass eye.
The day I was born she braided my living
sister's hair, walked my brother
to the outhouse and wiped him
and fed the chickens and milked the black cow.
She carried water in buckets
up steps from the spring house
to the stove, then down to the wringer washer
where dashers knocked, beating my father's

overalls clean. Two children at her knees
and one still rocking in her head
and one in her belly pushing.

SECOND SKIN

for the infant sister
who died the year I was born

Dost thou know who made thee?
... Gave thee clothing of delight,
Softest clothing woolly bright.
—William Blake, "The Lamb"

Yes I know whose pelt I wore
those first few hours,
whose woolly death covered me,
a sheep in sheep's clothing—

for I've seen an orphan
at lambing time, tottering
in a borrowed cloak,
suck the teat

of a dead lamb's mother.
My shepherd friend tells me
how this trick is turned:
with a knife he unzips

the carcass of the dead lamb,
which peels off in one piece,
tail and all, even the sack
of each slippered foot,

all the way to the muzzle
and the twin leaves of ears,
a perfect body stocking
that fits neatly over

the orphaned lamb
who, now doubly warmed,
twice blest, wobbles on new legs
across the blood-dried straw

where the mother waits,
her womb still slack
from its recent emptying.
The miracle, my friend says,

is how easily she takes
the lost one for her own.
A quick sniff, a nuzzle,
and the milk ducts answer,

while the lamb, already
itching to shed the jacket
of the dead, fastens itself
to the rubbery teat

and the mother gives in,
her black eyes staring
dumbly at the burial field
pocked with stones.

THE LANDSCAPE OF MY GRANDMOTHERS' NAMES

for Golda Groves and Sylvia Mounts

Silver and gold rings worn thin on knotted
roots of their fingers. Between them
a century of married nights, starched gowns
and the everpresent slop jar beside the bed.
In the east window, heat lightning is building,
then suddenly the flash, gray sky releasing
its earned metallic anger like the taste of blood
in my grandmother's mouth that summer
decades before I was born, the single gold filling
she dug from a tooth and redeemed
for flour and lard. Or like rust on my lips
from the morning's first dipper of well water
pumped by a grandmother's arm.
When I dream them it is always summer.
The smell of sweat and the yeasty rise
of bread in metal pans. I stand between them,
cool and safe in the shade of their lives.
For them, only flat and flatter fields,
soybeans and corn, row upon row,
perfectly even, white sun bleaching
the wide spaces between. No grove to hide in,
no mountain from which to view
the scene from higher ground. One grandmother
climbed a stallion, rode out her fears
on his back. The other cooled her rage
in icy creeks, hip-deep in minnows.

From eaves and gutters the rainwater trickled
into barrels to be collected for the Saturday
rinsing of daughters' hair, eight daughters

between them, not counting the ones
marked by hand carved stones. Not counting
the granddaughters and great-, who keep coming
years past my grandmothers' deaths
entangling like vines into one large death
and all the details confused. Golda laughed
her last words to a daughter who lifted her
from the bed. *Look what earth does to us!*
she said, meaning what was left
of her flesh as it spilled over the bedpan.
Sylvia was silent at the end, hands folded
across her breasts, still beautiful even at ninety.

In the only picture of them together
they are standing on a makeshift airfield
on either side of my pilot father who guides
an elbow of each. *Mother*, he called one. *Mom*,
the other, and this flight is a gift, their first
and last time *up*. Their housedresses are fluttering
around their knees, chiffon scarves tied
over their tarnished hair. Behind them
the propeller spins its dangerous circle.
Soon both will laugh at how quickly—considering
their combined weights—the plane lifts
from the ground. Both will look down
without fear, surprised to see how small
everything is, how well their lives continue
without them: the fields and plow horse,
tiny dots of grandchildren emerging
from the barn, the stream only this morning
engorged with rain and the promise of trout,
now a thin ribbon, insignificant as the loose
thread a child discovers and pulls and pulls,
amazed at how easily it all comes undone.

A Woman Like a Corner House

opens herself to all
directions. Where street signs
tangle, she searches her name.
She owns no secrets, her backyard
a public stage. Gowns on the
clothesline. Garbage, metal
lips of cans clinking.

Late night men in passing
cars leave trails of empty
bottles. To children she is
a shortcut, a way to get
to there. They wear
her grasses low. She is the elbow
leaning on itself, dreaming
a place with no curves or
turns, where corners untie,
slip from their knots, unwinding
to pure straight line.

MARINE BASE

Balancing barefoot
on unpacked crates,
she remembers his promise:
the best thing about a Quonset hut
is the artillery rain on
metal roof. But here the sky
coughs its brown throat. Dust.
Dry heaves. And Mother hangs
a picture of waves
on curved tin walls. She tacks
each corner to keep the waves
from spilling off the canvas,
drowning her youngest
sleeping on the foldout couch.

Outside on the jungle gym,
we play kamikaze
games of dead man's drop,
balance on iron bars, throw
back our bodies until they
snap. Now hinged by skinny knees,
we hang upside down,
our eyes swimming the green
of the general's house on the hill.
We dangle, a row
of question marks. Our hair
brushes the khaki dirt.

X

Summers over tic-tac-toe I crossed out
whole afternoons, slow to see
that X marks the place where victims fall
as well as buried treasure. Years later in school

I learned a blond hair from an Iowa woman
formed the cross-sight for Hiroshima.
When I questioned my father, he nodded
slightly, sadly, and kept on plotting

the quadrants of my algebra homework,
tracing for the third time that night
the puzzling intersection of x and y. *One
chromosome,* my friend is saying. *That's all it takes.*

We are sitting outside in old-fashioned
lawn chairs that press against the backs
of our thighs, forming an intricate latticework.
Inside the house, beneath the marionette strings

of a circus mobile, her baby sleeps,
his slanted eyes and dry fissured lips
linking him to thousands of genetic brothers,
and I think of childhood Bible Schools,

the missionary banner—"Christ for the World"—
stretching from the wooden pulpit
to the earth's four corners. Once I stood
in four states at once. My mother still has the photo.

There I am, seven years old, splayed like a starfish:
a hand in Colorado, another in Utah, one leg each
in Arizona and New Mexico. Around us miles
of turquoise sky where a hundred years before,

smoke from tepees rose. *Everything
an Indian does is in a circle*, the great
Sioux chief said. *Everything tries to be round.*
Documentary cameras were clicking. He stood

inside a square reservation house and pointed
to the corners, saying *That is why we died.*
My grandfather's last month was measured
in x's of the fence he hammered

on the farthest acre of his land, while upstairs
my grandmother collected x's in her lap,
canceling the empty muslin with thread and needle,
one stitch by one stitch, until a flower bloomed.

SNOW WOMAN

In childhood's first flurry,
we never thought to build a woman.
Three small sisters

in woolen gloves, patting
together the perfectly
sexless, three-part man.

Stiff twig arms, the frozen smile.
Even Father's hat stolen from the shelf
did not make him ours.

Today in first snow
we are grown-up sisters
on our way to build a woman.

The eldest, stooped from sudden weight,
carries a daughter on her back.
The youngest carries hers in her belly.

What falls from the sky
is white and pure.
We catch it on our tongues.

If we could, we would build her whole.
Start at the head—pristine
features, a thoughtful nod.

But it can't be done. Our woman
requires a sturdy base.
Earth is the place to begin.

We pack the snow between
our hands, lower it to the ground,
gently roll it round.

Her body grows in our hands.
And as we roll, earth attaches itself—
twigs, branches, leaves.

We struggle, lift her upright in the snow,
kneel to carve the first space.
Her thighs spread wide,

we crawl on all fours
through the place where we began.
We pad more snow: the hills

of her buttocks. Too small a waist
and she would crumble,
we build her rounded there.

The breasts we build are Mother's
breasts. Shoulders broad,
back strong. And now the neck,

the stem we pray
will hold. Tomorrow she will be gone,
yet we fashion her as if

she were forever. Grandmother's
mouth, full lips and laughing.
The nose of our dead sister.

And for her eyes, an aunt
we never knew except in stories.
They say one eye was brown,

fixed straight ahead or slightly down.
The other was blue with a mind of its own,
gazing a bit toward heaven.

PARDON

May I be excused? I ask from the breakfast table,
and Mother scans my plate. The clock
above my head sweeps its black hand,
but nothing is cleaner. Outside on the street
my friends plod their Saturday road to confession.
So much to haul, and I too want to spill it
to the deep voice behind the curtain
while Mother Mary looks on, condoning again
for one more week, my entire plate of sin.
But I am Baptist. My salvation, one public wringing
that had to take, the choir singing "Just As I Am,"
as I ask *May I be excused?* to Jesus,
who lifts his dying head, the crown of thorns,
and nods just once before his last words,
and I carry that nod the rest of my days,
like the wilted lunch bag I fold and bring home
each day to Mother. Years later
in the back seats of cars when the warm tongues of boys
lap up the memory of that ancient forgiveness,
I see them again, my Catholic friends
floating back from confession, the accordion
pleats on their skirts like a sheaf of new leaves
turning over, their patent leather shoes
immaculate, the sun on their backs like a pardon.

Missionary

Not the position you take with a man,
but the real calling you first hear
over ocean waters or sitting in church
and before you know it you're bringing home strays.
At five, Alice LaConte from the apartments,
her lice hitchhiking in your hair. All night
your mother scrubs, muttering, *Your friends, honey,
your friends,* but the zeal is just beginning
and by first grade you're bringing them for dinner,
their scabs and ticks and ringworm
infecting the whole family, so for weeks
you must all drink black syrup and change
underwear three times a day. In junior high
it's Melinda with the limp, first time up
you choose her for your tennis partner
and thank her for the opportunity. In high school,
it's *you* he loves, Bo Pederson
with the stuttering eye reflecting the ghosts
of the parents he stabbed, but you see only
the bright flower of his need, so of course
in college it's the broken one you want,
the hood who has slept six nights
in his jacket, your first date is to the bank
where you withdraw prematurely your entire
savings to pay for some brown-eyed girl's abortion,
so that night he sits across a booth from you
and writes a rhyming poem about a blue-eyed
saint who loves him in spite of, and because
that's what you've been training for,
by June you're kneeling at the altar

(as close to China as you'll ever get) and finally in bed
when you take the missionary position,
it's an orgy, it's the whole unwashed mob you love,
sure you will sustain them forever so you're astonished
to wake and find them gone without a thank-you,
him and that multitude of sinners
you've been courting all these years.

BRIDAL RITES

I sniff for hot coals, search
the sweaty firelit circle of women.
Around me they huddle, dimpled knees
pressed together to balance
Bride-Bingo cards. Stockings rub,
nylon heat rises. *B-7*, she shouts,
clacking dentures, and a murmur
like dishwater bubbles through the crowd.
Mother's cousin has won again,
two packages of colored clothespins.

I come barefoot to this passage,
hunting the one-eyed medicine woman
to lead me through the bloody breaking.
I want to ask how it feels.
Rough, his tongue, like a cat's on your skin?
Smooth? Do you slide together?
Where do his eyes go?
Do you remember? His scent,
does it stay in your hair?

They smile and bring me what they know:
yellow peignoir with uplift bra, vegematic,
tupperware. They caution me on leftovers,
how vital to keep the celery crisp.
We move to the table, where cashews
bed down with pastel mints. In the punch bowl,
dollops of sherbet float like breasts set free.
The women cut the cake into uniform slices.
Giggle. Snap my picture.

I leave heavy with their gifts.
In the distance, the ancient moon,
the she-wolf howling.

THE WORD

1. Daily Bread

With milk each morning
I cried for my word,
mouth open to catch
the wafer Mother dropped
on my hungry tongue.
I watched her teeth, straight
and white as the words she gave.
Her lips split apart,
her tongue flashed out
then suddenly in.
Light, she whispered, tugging
the switch up and down
until my eyes blinked in rhythm.
She taught me *water, saucer, yes.*
Shadow she would save.

Today I wake, hungry.
Say *grotto* to me, I beg.
You tease me with *seashell,*
starfish, crab. But I need *grotto,*
the grit on my teeth, the growl.
Last month it was *hollow*.
Everywhere I traced it.

2. In the Beginning

Here in this wind-swept cabin,
stripped of television and toys,

our nieces are making a language.
On their haunches they crouch
as if beside some ancient fire.
They rub their hands
and the first words spark:
Booca (bread.) *Itsa* (I).
Hot. Cold. Hungry.
Soon they shiver, reach for *you*,
join hands, dance in circles.

3. Love's Language

Not flowers. Not the simple
picture our nephew draws,
a rose opening soft as a sigh
to the lily's insistent pistil.
When you come
it is more like going
and you clutch me to tether yourself
to earth, swinging out, out
to the blackness of in.

4. Grandmother, After the Stroke

There was nothing left to say
after she called the porch a cemetery.
Her signals bred hybrids.
Now slippers are catacombs
and Ruth is Marge.

5. Voice Lesson

Somewhere you lost it
and must find it again,
the voice you were born with.
When the wind starts,
your strings will vibrate.
Now, begin. On your back.
Pant like a puppy
until the whole cage
expands. Contracts. Expands.
You are a newborn,
cords of elastic,
chin loose as butter.
We will begin again.

II

GHOST, KISS

...the two most powerful words in the infant-room vocabulary, under any circumstances: ghost, kiss...

—Sylvia Ashton-Warner,
from *Teacher*
on teaching kindergarten
to the Maori children of New Zealand

Salvage

for a dead sister

I wore the bonnet knitted for you,
the hooded gown, your diapers
still folded on the dresser. *Congenital,*
the grown-ups said when I finally asked:
it was your heart that undid you.
The world you left, I used sparingly.
I crumbled soap slivers into the washcloth,
dug with a toothpick the last smear
of lipstick. Forty years, and still I haunt
the aisles of secondhand stores, past
bins of blouses, trousers torn and mended,
shelves of pointed pumps I squeeze
my feet into. Here, a stone dug in
too long. A run-down heel. And hobble
in some stranger's shoes home
where my husband—who came complete
with ex-wife and son—waits for me,
his face softening like a leather glove
worn just long enough. Dinner-time,
I pull from the bureau an old quilt
and spread it across the table.
Now where someone's feet
once rested, there is this plate.

INFANT HILL, ELMWOOD CEMETERY

In the cartography of grown-up plots, six feet
the measure of a man, it is difficult to fit
a playpen fence, expensive to mow the uneven spaces
between. So on this hillside between public housing's
dusty porches and the interstate, the babies
are planted together. A truck rumbles past,
bequeathing to the asphalt slab the wrappings
of a tire outlasting its second chance.
On the fence, honeysuckle and wild roses
entangle in the perennial lust of summer
and a young girl walks the frontage road alone,
her hand resting on a white shirt shrouding
a belly that has swelled beyond expectation.
It is always a surprise, the seed that sprouts.
Always a surprise to bury an infant. What we mourn
is a heart that had barely stuttered, a blossoming
petal of lung, yet we must name him someone,
if only Infant Son of Sharon and Tim. Any more
might sink the memory deep as these stones
promising too much: John Fitzgerald, Malcolm,
George Washington Carver the Fourth.
The newer graves are a comfort, soap opera's
brief bubble—Tiffany, Brittany, Jeremy, Hope,
names interchangeable as this row of identical
stone lambs grazing atop graves weedy with forgetfulness.
And here is a death too fresh for a marker, only
this clutch of blue carnations and a day old helium balloon
with a few breaths left, an exhausted valentine
someone stood in line at the grocery store to buy.

LAMENT

How do I mourn
what barely was—

tadpole legs
swimming my sea,

pulse a muffled
watch's ticking

years too late,
this space that grows

deep below
my girlish breasts,

below my stomach
flat as this day,

flat as the name
stuck in my throat—

Rachel or Hannah
or Anna Kathleen,

my tiny seed,
my never girl.

Somewhere in Iowa, a Woman

leans over steaming pots,
over the soft flesh of plums,
skins slipping off in her hands.
Her hair clings damp, curling
on her cheek, a woman giving
birth all over again. Her breath
fogs the window. She calls their names.
Her daughters, years gone.

From faded pictures, Mona,
her name like dark honey
poured across the tongue.
When they told her, she kept right on
sprinkling each tiny dress.
The iron hissed in nests
of small puffed sleeves.
She pressed lace collars,
finished, untied her apron.
Stacked the dresses, flat and dry,
at the end of the ironing board.

And Deborah. Horses pulled
the wagon, plow horses harnessed
to a lighter task, this wooden casket
that might have been a tool box,
but nothing inside rattled.
In a flannel gown she stood
by the window, watching
the awkward horses pass, their breath
frozen silver on the muzzles.

TWIN

Animals in their dumb wisdom
eat the placenta. Ancient Egyptians
worshipped it, preserved it at birth
to bury years later with the body, fearful
it would wander unmoored, forever
in search of its double. Doctors say
sometimes the placenta refuses to be born
and must be scraped away, dragging
with it the carpet of future children.
But usually it follows obediently
on our heels, this cake of blood
and memory, blind to the first light
we blink back. And when they cut it from us
and the seal of our mouth is broken,
maybe the cry that rises is a goodbye
to the sister who knew us when.
Before the quickening, before heartbeat
or fingernail, when we swung
dreamily from the other end
of a blue-veined rope, joined once and only
with our twin. Wholly nothing, whole.

Burial

Like a sister who borrows
a blouse without asking,
the earth slipped

the ring from my finger
as I worked the soil
that spring

when your leaving
was a seed planted
beneath my knowing.

I dug among roots,
white tendrils, my emptied
hand snaking deep.

Months later
when the seed sprouted
there was nothing

left of you to remove.
The bare finger
wore the shape

of absence, pale
ring of flesh the sun
was slow to touch.

Staining the Porch Rocker

I would have left it as it was.
Pale, newly shaven.
Nails poking their heads
through the innocent pine.
The sun would have bleached it
to buckling, the rains
softened it to destruction,
a sweet rotting where ants
and termites make their home.
I have always been one
to love a natural aging.

But you left too soon,
and alone that night
I found a dozen reasons.
My hands were bare.
The stain oily, thick.
I stroked the arms,
the hard back, the slats
driven fast together.
Even the spaces beneath,
the spaces no one sees,
I rubbed, my hands
on the bare wood
darkening.

Ex-Brother-in-Law

Without the law, there is no brother,
and no ceremony to mark the breaking.
Christmas Eve from the box packed away last year
we uncover the stocking stitched with your name,
not knowing what to do with it. Later as we gather
to watch family slides projected on a sheet,
your face surfaces among ours, miraculous
as the imprints emerging on the shroud of Turin.
When you were here, how simple it seemed,
the pattern of blame and solution: If only you would turn
that way or this, if only you would disappear,
my sister's life could begin again. But what of *our* lives,
the severed sisters, aunts, brothers, nephews, nieces,
fathers, mothers—all those unregistered
couplings of hearts—left to wonder
if you were ever ours, and by what decree.

Have you married some new family, are you sharing
their holiday feast while we sit here
at the table you refinished—your windburnt hands
with the freckled knuckles, rough-hewn hands
that sanded until the grain revealed itself,
the complicated whorls beneath the surface
where so much of you remains. The daughter
you started fourteen years ago wears your face
and keeps growing. And your son still brags
about the time you accidentally shot a power-driven
nail through your hand while building
a skate ramp—*For me!* he sings proudly. *For me!*

It's the small things that make a job,
you once said as you knelt eye-level to the task:
this cabinet you built to store the mementos,
all the odd, unmatched relics that have no place.
You worked two days and we were satisfied.
No, you said, *it's the finishing that matters*.
Another day's labor found its completion:
a hand sanded notch and this perfectly engineered
sliding latch with its effortless closing and opening.

Neighbors

Last night while we slept the sound
sleep of the long married,
the couple next door moved out,
leaving the remnants of their quarrel
strewn beside the curb for the morning
pick-up: broken slats from a director's chair,
a few old albums, some cardboard boxes
I was tempted to open. When they moved in—
two young men—they planted
a garden that thrived beyond logic,
as if some horticultural secret
were buried in the soil. Their garden grew
bloodroot, stepbrother to Sweet William.
Purple coleus with corduroy leaves,
impatiens sprouting glorious pinks and corals.
July mornings while I bent in the heat
to pinch back the chrysanthemum's
premature bloom, the lovers lounged
in silk pajamas on a sofa they'd carried
to the porch, plumped with cushions.
Music, old enough to mean something,
crackled from a phonograph whose cord
snaked through an open window.
I paused on my knees to listen, recalling
the face and hands of a man I briefly loved.
When October turned over its old leaf,
my mums opened on schedule
their tight fists, while next door
tall stems, grown too fragile
to support the heavy heads of bloom,
bowed over grass littered with leaves.

The neighbors took the dog, but left
the chain rusting on a wooden deck
whose gaps are now packed with acorns
and seeds. They took the fountain
in the shape of a boy balanced precariously
on one perfect foot. Between us we shared
a brick wall, an alley that accessed
our back gates, and the generous trunk
of a hackberry tree whose limbs
reached into our separate yards.
They left a birdbath open to the sky.
If someone doesn't turn it to the ground,
come January it will glaze over
with a brilliant silver sheen
and crack in the first hard freeze.

Visit With the Newlyweds

She does not know how white her neck,
or how naked. He cannot pass her
without touching. It is summer,
their cotton clothes soft as gauze.
The relatives have given gifts
they will grow into. China teacups.
Glass birds. A clock with a second hand.
I have brought Sweet Williams.
She is amazed something so pink
can bloom every year without planting.
Yes, I answer. *Eleven years for us.*
Eleven? she asks and looks at the clock
as if everything were told in hours.
Upstairs by their bed, the wedding pillow.
Every night they marry again.
I want to tell them how crowded
the bed will become, how soon
he will sleep with her mother.
The bride yawns, her eyes
turning back the sheet.
Back home the sheets are thin,
the roses worn smooth
beneath bodies so familiar
we wear our skin like clothes.
You touch me and I move to lower
the straps I pretend are there.
Some nights I forget we are married.
Some nights it is all I know.

THE LOUD FAMILY

Across the empty space of these hills,
it's hard to keep secrets from your neighbors,
especially in summer, windows open
to the bullfrog's swampy bellow, the racket
of birds whose names we don't know.
My husband and I are city people who own
a piece of this place, and until last year
our neighbors were a splash of local color,
laughable as a cartoon family. We named them
The Louds, everything bigger than life.
The father, all paunch and swagger,
a hunting rifle over his shoulder,
two small boys running behind him calling,
"Deddy, can we go? Can we?" And the retriever,
having recently emptied another round
of puppies onto the dirt floor of her pen,
would trot the road between our houses,
her teats sloshing wildly. The Loud mother,
a baby girl slung across her hip, waved
from the second-floor porch where she stood
gazing at the satellite dish as if it were
some giant moon, her raspy voice
scraping against the evening, a sea chantey
turned lullaby. Nights after supper the only
light from their house was a blue flicker,
then that blasted metallic clamor—
can after can of sit-com laughter
opening at the windows of our cabin
where we sat caressing the slim necks
of Chardonnay glasses, or quietly
turning pages of biography and poetry,

entering the lives of those whose daily grunts
and wheezes had been distilled
into something finer, the way I sometimes
make love to my husband, trying not to let
my body get in the way, trying not to be
the way I once imagined The Louds, their bellies
slapping noisily together. So I was shocked
when a neighbor delivered the news:
the younger son had stepped on a sewing needle,
and his blood poisoned swiftly.
I'd never thought of Death and the Louds together,
could not have expected how fine a suture
Grief would stitch, how heavy
the silence that traveled the valley
between us. A year has passed, it's summer again,
and we've opened the windows. A buzz saw
shrieks, it's the father building a fence
so the little girl won't toddle too far.
Puppies are whimpering, a new baby daughter
is mewing, it's good to hear them at it again.
The mother hollers at the son who is left,
and I can tell by his whine he's happy
to be yelled at. Beneath the shadow
of the satellite dish, the retriever lifts her head
as if trying to trace a rustle in the grass, then
returns to her brood, licking their sealed eyes.

A Bath

for William Matthews

Not much, just
everything: white tiles,
liquid mirror, the room asteam.
I soap each crease, each plumped
exuberance. My friend is dead. Long
live my friend. His bones were large
and gangly. He limped into rooms.

I pumice the rough spots:
elbows, knees. The hinges
are first to go—at every juncture,
a separation. The last time I saw him
he left his overcoat at the table
and had to reclaim his steps.
Why bother, I wondered.
Old coat, limp and gray
as his mustache, his face,
the pockets of flesh beneath
his eyes. The body is too much

with us. The bath water clouds—
soap shavings, infinitesimal
bits of skin. Man became mortal,
the ancient ones said, because he refused
to shed. My friend slipped his arms
into the coat, his big hands
nervous for a cigarette.
He kept watching the clock.

The last train to the city, he said.
I paid for the wine, three
glasses and he was gone.

Another Cancer Poem

for Carolyn Schirmer

Hold it up to the light:
My friend left the print of her body
on the white sheet spread for her.
The corners were not even.
These words are not her cries.
She exhaled the breath of old books,
brittle pages a browser leafs through.
I apologize for the metaphor, but she loved books.
Pages a browser *leafs* through, then *leaves*.
I promise not to use any more metaphors.
When I lifted her hand, light webbed
the spaces between her fingers.

This Side

for Melanie Peter

Early on, your passion was The Nude,
your paintings a delight of flesh
gone to flesh, the sag and droop
of gravity seducing our bodies back
to earth. *It's flesh we are drawn to,
drawn from,* you said. The last time
I saw your son alive, he was fourteen
and already you were moving
past the canvases of skin and substance.
I want to see through *this world,*
you said, *and it makes me tired.*

"The roar on the other side of silence,"
one artist called this place, warning
that we could die from it, from seeing
the grass grow, hearing the squirrel's
heart beat. In your new paintings
secret folds unfolded, crevices turned
inside out. An Ohio cornfield relinquished
its still life to the rumble between the stalks
until your own ears turned inward
and you heard the yellow silks
whispering a rumor of rain. Somewhere
on the undersides of leaves, your son
was lost, the only link a long-distance
connection once a month or so
when he called begging for the money
that would rock him into some other world.
And when he quietly let go of himself

three days before Easter, you agreed
to cremation, watching the smoke
and believing that if the water stayed
still enough, the ashes you scattered
like seeds might one day sprout.
But lost is one thing. Gone, another.
I wish I'd taken a picture of his body,
you say, surprised that what you miss
is not what lies on the other side.
Yesterday for the first time in weeks
your stomach betrayed you with hunger
and you were angry that your body
was moving so soon back. You stood
in the kitchen, his clothes laid out
on the ironing board where you sifted
through them, the weekly duty
any mother might perform, pulling
from her son's dungarees the leavings
of a school day—nothing much, a few coins,
a wad of lint, a love note folded
and creased so many times it has grown
small and hard enough to be a weapon
that aimed just right and thrown with enough
velocity, might put someone's eye out.

In the Face Of

for Ann Hood

Because we are not made of stone
and grief is not the end of us
(though we have begged that it be so)

your face is not the finished mask
a sculptor carves, as if to say
Here, forever, is the face

of a mother who has outlived a child.
And wouldn't that be high relief:
to build a face from outside in,

to strap it on, a plate of sorrow
fixed in time. *Bravery in the face of,*
someone once wrote, meaning the granite

face of death that stares us down,
eye upon eye, daring us to break.
Yet brave beyond brave, your face

breaks open to allow the world back in.
I watch it swim behind your eyes,
violently brilliant, flashing its fin.

And now the roar—the pitch and roll
of memory's waters, the shifting
pulse of daughter, mother. The quickening.

JULY 11

for Ellen Johnston-Hale

The day my friend died I ran
an extra mile   plugged my ears
with speakers to silence   the silence

slammed   one foot down   the other
down again   another mile   another
friend   Bill Paul Kent   Ellen

a death so fresh I can dial her number
and her voice will answer   *I'm not here*
right now   Leave me a message

and I wait for the beep (long beep   short)
drumbeat   heartbeat   little engine
that could   that could   that couldn't

and where do they go so fast without us
heartbeat   drumbeat   little engine
knocking inside my chest

The day my friend died   another
friend was born   forty years before
and soon would arrive

for the birthday dinner   so my heart
still knocking   I chopped
cabbage into thinnest

strands for the slaw Amy loves
and shucked the corn   and deviled
the eggs with just enough sting

and crowded the cake with years
then   taking my time   lit each one
and watched my living friend   fill

her lungs   and send
her breath across the cake
as flames burned down to wax

SONIC

Passing gardenias tinged at the edges
and weighted to fall, I slow my pace, and your voice,
dead friend, wraps around me. Before we met
in the flesh, as the saying goes, we met in the ear,
your voice pressing through phone wires, a sonorous
baritone. *This could mean trouble*, I remember thinking—
me whose married years had been mostly happy,
though that year was not among them.
If love is blind, I might as well be, too, falling as I do
first for a man's voice. All the men I've ever wanted
had voices like thunder or tunneled air
or water rushing over stone. Sometimes
when my husband speaks I close my eyes
to keep them from interfering. The tongue,
most muscular shrub, is planted in the hollow
where song is born, but that year his tongue
was silent as if rooted on both ends.

When Adam swallowed the apple, it lodged
in his throat. Thus the name for the corded knot
that bobbed as you spoke months later, in the flesh,
saying *We'd better not* (I've always chosen good men
to almost love) and you were right,
it would have been a knot we could not untie
so I let you go. I am trying to remember.
Bodies weren't the issue, and later when I showered,
it wasn't your scent that left my hands, my hair.
It was your voice, its pitch and roll, waves
rippling from the center of disturbance.

What happens to voices when the body is gone?
Are they locked into boxes like the growl
my mother removed from the stuffed bear
that so terrified my brother? *See*, she said,
lifting it delicately out. *That's all it was,*
just a little box. Nothing to be afraid of.
If death is the end, what to make of your voice
alive in this air? The ear is so needy,
scientists say, so bent on making wholeness
from broken sound, it supplies the missing
harmonies of a partly fingered chord.
Though you were barely mine, your voice goes on
and on in my head, refracting, bending into harmonic
constitutions that fall back on me, the way
a tremor traveling a taut rope returns
to the hand that sent it forth.

HELLO LOVE

She has sent these words into the future
to no one in particular. I find them
in next month's calendar planted on her desk.
My niece's handwriting loops back
on itself, each vowel so womanly
in its roundness, the o's might be eggs
or breasts, or the flower of an open mouth.
She has written *love*, not *lover*,
addressing the whole world of possibility.
And no comma separates the greeting
from the greeted: It is *hello love* she wants.
Her father is huge in his chosen absence,
growing larger each year she waits.

Not long ago, temporarily lost between
the goodbye and hello of a man
I had loved since before she was born,
I drove my niece up a mountain. I thought
it was time she saw the view, how small
our city from this height, how the shoulders
of the most impressive hills soften
when draped with fog. *It's okay*, she said.
Don't worry, he'll be back. On the way down
an approaching truck swerved, its drunken
headlights swimming, and I slammed my arm
across her chest—a mother's gesture,
inherited and useless—as if the laws of physics
alter for those we love. No matter this time.
We escaped with our lives, all our pasts
and futures hurtling toward us. At sixteen,
my hair like hers was long and heavy,

a luxurious burden I carried for love.
And when the boy left for no reason,
I sliced off the hair and hid in my room,
a Rapunzel with no means of escape.
My father, home from Vietnam,
knocked and entered, his eyes downcast
as if he were the one responsible.
I expected to hear *We love you*,
the knot of words he kept in his throat
and untied in times like these.
Instead he gave the difficult pronoun,
claiming me as his own. My answer
was to turn and throw myself onto the bed.
In that moment I would have traded
seven fathers for the boy who was gone.
What I meant to say to my niece
as the valley beneath us dissolved in mist
was that hello almost never spells love.
There is room in the hollows of goodbye
for a full grown woman to hide.
The first man who left me was not my father.
Yet still I fall again and again in love
with the backs of men. And it will be a long time
before the face opening toward her
is more beautiful than the one turning away.

KNOWING HOW MY SUNS DIE

We argued all night
and into morning, which I called *next*
but you called simply *morning*.
No such thing as endings, you said.
Everything is round, repeats itself,
so when you see a bird disappear
into the west, if you sit in that place
long enough, watchful,
you will see the same bird
emerge in the east like the sun.

Speaking of birds, I interrupted.
You call them free but if you're right
they are caught in their closet of blue,
doomed forever to move their wings.
And, back to suns, I continued.
I have always believed every sun is new,
birthed red in the east each morning,
stretching its life across the sky
to die in the west that night.
I have always believed what I see.

Then you called me Columbus,
threw back your head and laughed
my ignorance to the ceiling
where I said it falls to the carpet to die
but you said it lives, reverberating,
bouncing back, floor to ceiling
to floor, always alive in the spaces
I cannot reach with my hands.

No, I argued, shaking my head.
I have always believed what I see.

So when you left I cried *Don't go!*
knowing how my suns die.
I watched you turn, and the laughter
you threw over your shoulder
I prayed would bounce from you
to me to you. I have sat in this place
so long, wanting to be wrong.
Look how still I sit, trying to feel
the dizziness there must be
if it's true, if we are truly spinning
and it's all one, all true
that we spin back like your one sun,
the one you swear always returns.

She Wanted to Leave a Great Emptiness Behind

In the house she would leave all the fullness
she could stir: sauces bubbling, white tents
of bread rising in the pan. Peonies perfect
in the vase, and below, the polished oak.
Cushions plumped, his brandy poured, coating
the petalled glass. And she would leave
her garden in all its wildness: fence vines
climbing the difficult ascent, purple
tangle of morning glory, so it might seem
it all thrived greener where her hands had been.
Then in the swell of the moment she would be gone,
leaving the great emptiness. And regret
would pile deep in his lap as plums.
And when he steered mourners through the halls
bare with her absence, he would mumble
but when she was here, and they would nod.

Do not question why she wanted this.
Truth is the strange cat outside our door
that will not come in lest we name him
and soften his color with our cream.
That is the way with truth, our mouths
on the thermos cannot see, only taste
the sweet or bitter when blind it enters
our throats. To spill is to waste its secret.
And departure wears its own perfume, aging
as it is born: doilies yellowed at the edge,
peonies bowing, fine talcum of dust.
Even the white mites fluttering the blossoms
could be her kiss. Together perhaps they wrote
this ending. Or some other hand floating

the spaces between. It could be worse.
Recall the warm socket when a tooth is gone.
You tongue the bruise, remembering.
So in the garden finally he might know her
as he sits alone on the marble bench.
Moss on the cherubs weaves a shawl,
and even the smallest rose dying
leaves a cavern rain hollows out,
where roots once made their bed.

III

SUN, MOON, STAR, PEARL

The Universe has everything.
That's what I like about it.

—James Galvin,
"On Exploration"

SIDEKICK

This one is for Barney Fife and Barney Rubble,
for Ed and Trixie, for Ethel and Fred,
the straight man, ploy, the wooden decoy bobbing,
back-up singers with their benign doo-wops,
and the boy in the back of the choir
who is asked to just please mouth the words.
For the runner-up without whom there could be no race,
the pageant princess who will never be queen,
Miss Congeniality, the bridesmaid clutching for an instant
the white bouquet, perennial benchers suited up
in virginal uniforms, the ones off whom the light bounces,
moons to the first sun, the eclipsed girl walking the beach,
the one who packs the lunches, the one whose order
the waiter keeps forgetting, and all those casino singers
from One-Hit-Hotel, spinning dizzily on the same old song,
forty five revolutions per minute for the rest of their lives.

Once I dreamed a show where no one was a star,
the cast a chorus of could-have-beens—
the envelope-opener at the Oscars, the virtuoso's
page turner, the understudy who broods each night
wingless in the wings, second-string violins, second sons,
the side of the face the camera never sees,
the big zero, placeholder, goose egg
hatching all the other numbers. First drafts, shed skin,
the flayed remains of St. Bartholomew, the chaff
and fodder, papery husks the poem wriggles out of,
the scaffolding, first skeleton dismantled,
pencil sketches, gesture studies, the armature and cantilever
supporting the ubiquitous clay, plaster molds
wasted in the service of the bronze, the slave buried

alive with her king, the discarded placenta—
first nourisher, first to go—first wives who train
their husbands to be husbands for second wives.
Exhausted breath trailing the departing car.

There are blue back roads we will never travel, slender
capillaries feeding the big red vein that feeds the heart,
unvarnished undersides of desks that will never know
the tender violence of our graffiti. Folds of skin
untouched by sun or hand, also the undiscovered pearl,
the veiled beauty, the hidden knees of nuns
who bare themselves only on the flip side of dream
in that one brief encore, the curtain call
uncalled for until now when suddenly the silence
of one hand clapping is multiplied by thousands
of one-hands-clapping, calling all the sidekicks
back to the stage—the frame bursting its picture,
torn envelopes healing themselves, the sealing wax
once broken for the words inside, now sealing
a love letter to itself, the echo in the valley
composing its first song, Peter Pan's shadow peeling free,
Bartholomew's recovered body-stocking zipping itself
back together, topped by all the hats Rembrandt painted over
in his search to find himself, while below,
those hordes of idle shoes recovered from the closets
of amputees, are kicking up their smooth black heels.

Produce Aisle

The artichoke keeps her distance.
She has been taken too many times. Now
the armadillo armor hides her secret heart.

Everyone counts on the onion, staple of stews
and pottage. But deep in the crowded bin, her skin
is thin as moth wing. It peels away before their eyes.

Green peppers are modern women who take
their muscles seriously. They hunch their shoulders,
broad, shiny beneath a fluorescent sun.

Close by in cellophane the carrots keep
for weeks, the last to lose their figures. All legs,
tapering to slim ankles—and above,

wild profusion of hair. They gather in knots
of conversation and whisper about the apples,
those aging showgirls who didn't know when to quit,

redheads buffed an unnatural blush, a shine
that shouts *forever* while inside the white flesh softens.
In the center aisle, bananas in bunches

curl like firm young girls in sleep. Soon they will turn
like their half-price sisters, learn the bruise,
dark print that begins beneath the skin and grows.

Oh to be the avocado! She ages so well.
Time makes love to her daily, finding her sweeter
the softer she grows. Beside her the potato,

peasant woman in brown, comes into her own slowly.
She stays in the shadows, blindly remembers
her place. *Come to me! I will make you whole!*

coos the eggplant mother. And from the corner bin
a chorus: *Oranges, Oranges, Oranges, Oranges.*
We are what we seem. We speak our own name.

Something Calling My Name

There are times when I really miss it. I wish I had some dirt right now.
—Fannie Glass, a clay-eater, who has been off dirt
for over a year, at her husband's request.

I try to tell him. But he won't hear.
Earl, I say, it's safe, it's clean
if you dig below where man has been,
deep to the first blackness.
I tell him. But he won't hear.
Says my mouth used to taste like mud,
made him want to spit.

I try to tell him how fine it was.
When I was big with Earl Junior and Shad,
I laid on my back, my belly all swelled
like the high dirt hills
sloping down to the bank
above the gravel road by Mama's.
And I'd dream it. Rich and black after rain.
Like something calling my name.

I say Earl, remember? That spring in Chicago,
I thought I'd die, my mouth all tasteless,
waiting for Wednesdays, shoeboxes
full of the smell of home.
The postman, he'd scratch his head,
but he kept on bringing. Bless Mama.
She baked it right, the way I like.
Vinegar-sprinkled. And salt.
I'd carry it in the little red pouch
or loose in my apron pocket

and when the day got too long and dry
and Earl home too late for loving,
I'd have me a taste. It saved me, it did.
And when we finally made it back,
the smell of Alabama soil
poured itself right through me.
I sang again and things were fine
till the night he leaned back and said
No More, his man-smells all rich
and mixed up with evening. Right there,
laying by me, he made me choose
between his kisses and my clay.

Now afternoons when it gets too much,
I reach for the stuff he gave me.
Baking soda. Starch. I've tried it all.
But I don't hold with it.
It crunches good, but it's all bleached out
and pasty. It just don't take the place.

Earl, I say, I've given it up.
And right then, I have.
But sometimes on summer nights like this
when the clouds hang heavy
and I hear that first rumble and the earth
peels itself back and the crust darkens
and the underneath soil bubbles up
damp and flavored, it all comes back
and I believe I'd do anything
to kneel at that bank
above the gravel road by Mama's
and dig in deep till my arms are smeared
and scoop it wet to my mouth.

CENTRAL PARK: A CHRISTENING

One of those tired December
afternoons between holidays, a toss-up
of how to name it. Train your eyes
on the pond duck's glistening tail?
Or on the milky scum, the necks of bottles
marooned in shallows, beside the tattered
man with a voice large and round as God's
who stands by the water calling out
Ferdinand, Isabella, Tinkerbell, Cocaine,
Mona Liza (with a *z*, like the broken
singer), *Al Capone*—the way you'd call
scattered children home for dinner,
pausing at each one to allow
an answering echo. *Rockefeller, Sinatra,*
Vagina, John of Bede, Picasso, Marijuana,
Saint Teresa, Trump. And who is this blonde
in a fur coat, hurrying past on her way
somewhere? He falls into step
beside her, reaching out his hand,
not as a beggar—empty palm toward heaven—
but like a longtime husband, easy as air,
as if it were the most natural
thing in the world to offer your hand
to the woman you love, guide her
lightly around the puddle.

Autobiography of the cab driver who picked me up at a Phoenix hotel to catch a four a.m. flight and began to speak in (almost) rhyming couplets

I got two problems. One,
I never see the sun
and two, if I did,
I couldn't take it, never could.
Now, my sister? Out one day
and brown the next. That's the way
my father was. We never
took vacations but he used to steer
on Sundays with one arm
out the window. Get dark as a black man.
Something in his blood, I guess.
Once I bought me a mess
of tanning cream, but something
kept me from using it.
He's been dead a whole
year. They say there's not a soul
on the streets this hour,
but the souls are just now rousing.
Yes Ma'am, when I see daylight I slide
into my coffin and close the lid.
Cooler that way. They say if you can survive
a summer in this heat, you're a native.
My brother's child? She claims to be one,
but I tell her she's got Made in Japan
stamped all over her keister.
Hey lady, you still on Eastern
time? You can have it. Yesterday
the TV reporter in Cincinnati

was three feet in snow. I phoned
my old drinking buddy back home
to rub it in. Lied and said I was out
today without a shirt. Barefoot.
He said you can keep those hundred
degrees. I said you don't have to shovel
a heat wave. Young lady, you okay?
Looks like you're fading. The longest day
I ever lived was the night
I left for Vietnam. What a sight,
would you look at that? Damn
jackhammers at three a.m.
They sure like to play in the dirt here.
Yes Ma'am. It's the same everywhere.
The shortest distance between
two points is always under construction.

Good Fences

Mornings like this I am grateful
for thin blue lines that separate. I know why
the asylum inmate, when handed a sheet of paper, writes
his name as close to the edge as possible. God
himself moved early toward margins. Lost in galaxies
of pure freedom, the first motherless child cried out
to the terrible dark. How good it must have felt
when that first word found its shape. Stopped. Cleared
a space for the next, and next. *Let   there   be   light!*
sweet baby talk of creation. And what a surprise
when chaos obeyed, split in two, the first neighborly
fence between night and day. Now there was something
to lie in, something to wake to, that first watery morning.
Day poured itself around him. His head was swimming,
where to put it? So Heaven was born, first hint of *up*.
Down followed soon, his feet sucked toward Earth
where he rattled the first seeds into being, divided
the hairy clumps: Grasses. Trees. Herbs. Fruits.
Here was work to cut out for himself—sorting
the firmament into lesser and greater lights, the waters
into fish and fowl, into feather and fin, then the teeming
multiplications of beasts and men which are yet
recombining. No wonder he named the seventh day
Rest! and gasped to see what he had done.

HERA, GODDESS OF MARRIAGE

(from "The Seven Wives of Zeus")

Other men? I could have had them all.
Meteors ripen in the fold of my veil.
I'm Queen Of The Sky! The Milky Way
is the milk I spilled one day
as I suckled my child. Yes, hundreds of men!
More than the peacock eyes of Argus. (Once Ixion
embraced a cloud, thinking it was I.)
But from the beginning I set my eye
on *him*, the god of luminous ether.
I rule the lower, denser
air. We were meant for each other.
Don't even bother
counting other wives. I've blinded men for less.
(Ask Tiresias.)
You've heard us clattering about heaven,
throwing our weight around, his uneven
thunder, the zigzag revolt
of the lightning bolt
he slings at my crown. That's just his way
of loving me. You can say
what you will, a man wants an equal,
not a sequel
to himself. So understand this:
These chains on my wrists,
the iron bracelets, the anvils
on my ankles
can't hold me! Besides, I like this view.
It's all in the way you
look at it. Hanging upside-down

is not so bad, as long as your crown
stays put. It's staying power
that matters, from the first hour
on, past dragons and mistresses, past
disobedient children, you last,
live out all your lives with him:
Girl. Wife. Old woman.

One Flesh

Even in this spoon cradle
of sleep, his sex
pressed warm against you,

even in the near perfect
curve of a couple
grown almost into one,

there is this: the extra elbow,
the arm with no home.
Where do you put it?

Do you leave it here
beneath your head, until it falls
asleep, wakes heavy, tingling,

and you stare at it,
willing the fingers to move
as if they belonged to a stranger?

They say it is possible,
the perfect arc, two merging
flawlessly to one.

So for a moment you wish
it gone, this offending limb
with a mind of its own.

Why not fold it gently
into the bureau, between
the handkerchiefs and gowns

and dream the rest:
knuckles and knees
slide from their sockets

one by one.
Then his too. Ankles,
elbows, shoulder blades, spines

rise from your bodies
and stack themselves
white and glistening

beneath the window.
Basted with moonlight,
your bones and his,

while across the room
the two of you curl
boneless and soft,

becoming the *other*
like Bible couples
they told you about:

one flesh.
And you the wife: forsaking
all others, cleaving to him.

Coitus Hysterium

If some statistician were looking
on, charting the number of times
we up or down the national average,
this coupling might confuse him.
We are not the Joneses
or the Johnsons, simply masters
in the art of married laughter,
and another position we sometimes take
in love is flat on our backs,
spending ourselves in knee slaps
and shrieks to the bedroom wall.
We never intend to go this far,
but things get quickly out of hand,
out of even your brilliant hands
which after twenty-plus years never
fail to answer my body's questions.
(Your slightest tug can make me
dance and throw my voice so far it may
still be singing somewhere!)
So this is not counting, certainly
not *dis*counting the seamier joys
of married trysts, those permutations
of pleasure one man and woman take
and give. Nor the times when loss
has lashed us together and we've wept
at the lastness of things, washing
ashore on broken bodies. Yes,
any shadow hovering recasts
the scenes below. But tonight let's not
praise the buzz saw of passion,

the thin edge that could razor
one couple into separate strands.
There's something to be said
for the thrust and rhythm
of a joke well told, the rolling
wave of a belly laugh solving
the body's other riddles.
Knock, knock, I whisper, breathless
in the silence I count on you
to break in two, your hands
in the dark moving beyond lust
to cup the answer, the quilled
titillation of your mustache against
my ear: *Who's there?*

Afterglow

for my first husband

When you left our new marriage for another woman's bed,
the sheets were still rumpled from unfinished loving.
I didn't know it would be our last try. Twenty years
since I've seen you, but lately I've been replaying the scene,
and since only in bed did we ever agree (and even then, clumsily)
I keep tucking us in, wishing to dream it right:
a one night, last chance reunion, the decades of dammed-up
guilt and regret pushing against our bodies until—
as they say in romance novels—we are flooded with passion.

When the dam finally breaks and the dream trickles through,
we're back in your teenage bedroom. The same fringed lamp,
the polished row of debate trophies, the chenille spread
your mother washed and fluffed each Saturday.
At the foot of the bed she's still fluffing,
and from the champagne bottle on the nightstand
your father effervesces, his head the cork popping.
Remember at the engagement party how he lifted his glass,
a toast of warning: *If you wonder how your wife*
will look in twenty years, just look at her mother.
Well darling, here I am. You, too, across the room of this dream,
wearing your father's timid hairline, his paunch blooming
over your belt buckle as you move to unlatch it.
Your parents fizzle as bubbles do, and we are left
surveying each other, our expressions forgiving, and more:
pride in the wisdom of early choices. *You look good,*
you've held up well, we say. *I always knew you would.*

The rest is coda. The bed, an appointment we must keep.
I would not name it passion. Perhaps it is the only gift
we know to give or take. We unwrap it the best we can,
coaxing out moans and when it is over, exhausted thanks.
What a relief to have it finished—the failures, the burden
that memory lays on us, the expectation of lust.
Just to lie here mildly amused, after all these years
finally postcoital. Grateful it was nothing, really.
Glad not to wake with my little finger
in my mouth, wet, still dreamy, wishing you back.

REGRETS ONLY

At the party to which only regrets are invited,
our pasts cluster on the front stoop
whispering *if only* and *what if*
and growing smaller with each telling
until we can squeeze through the tiny door
like the proverbial camel through the needle's eye,
a task made possible by sloughing off
the humped burden of riches. So we check it all
at the door—our late model joys, the second
husband and children, golden friends
with their promises to stand by—and enter alone.
Once inside, we don't lack for company.
Everyone we ever failed is there, and those
who failed us. Mr. Wrongs fill the mirrored hallway,
ghosts of first spouses mull around the table.
The platters are full. We feast on half-baked schemes.
Our scars gleam, and all the fine white stitches.
Miss Havisham holds court in cobweb finery
while her married sisters wear children for sleeves,
their bridal gowns spread like napkins
across their bountiful laps. If after all these years
the slipper still fits, don't wear it. Dress
inappropriately, if at all. Wear your dead mother's
blouse inside out, revealing the tattered lining,
or your father's hospital smock, open at the back.
In the scheme of things, this shame is nothing.
Look around. The hit-and-run driver
keeps backing herself into a corner, circling,
recircling the event. And the murderer
has grown hunchbacked carrying the weight.
At the party to which only regrets are invited,

we meet ourselves coming and going,
like the man in the childhood riddle whose life
multiplied seven times sevenfold by those he met
along the way—*kits, cats, sacks, wives,*
how many were going to Saint Ives? In truth,
he was the lone traveler. All along, the answer was *one*.

Need and Want in Late December

We blink our eyes
and another holiday careens
around the corner, trapping us
within its beam, stunning us motionless.
Time slows, our animal heart pounds—
there is something we should be doing,
and *now*, but all we can do is stare
into the haloed glare where a form
sits low, small in the driver's seat.
It is a child, it is our past wearing
clothes we thought we'd outgrown,
giddily innocent behind the wheel,
steering the new year toward us.

And why not a child?
Christmas is a child's birthday
party, and we all remember
how that went: someone was always crying,
someone was left out, someone's gift
was loved better than the next,
and no matter how many appeared
wearing their best hearts, there was always
the one who didn't show, the one
we kept watching the door to see.
Disappointment was the tail
we pinned on the donkey—or tried to,
but we were blind and dizzy
from spinning. Years pass, another game,
another blindfold, the piñata swinging
high, someone hands us a stick
and we flail, we pound

as if our lives depend on it,
wild for the papery beast to pour
its sweetness over our heads.

Miracles happen
this time of year, they say,
and make movies to prove it:
snow falls evenly on each gabled roof
while inside, a fire glows
to warm the empty stockings
(there's one for the dog too)
and even the most hardened child believes
the stocking stitched with his name
will fill. This is what I'm thinking
as I sit between two children
I've borrowed for the evening—
my need more than theirs.
We are watching a holiday movie
where everyone gets what they want,
which is the brightest lie of the season,
along with the songs: Christmas *isn't* a time,
it's a place, a crowded intersection
where all our needs collide. Today
in the department store I watched
a well-dressed man pull from his wallet
a stack of gold cards—
we all throw whatever we have
into the ring, maybe this time,
this year, we'll win. Chances are
a boy's heart thumps wildly
inside him: he's still waiting
for his mother to appear at the door,
or the phone to deliver
his father's voice to his ear,

or he's afraid that once again he will fail
to give what she wants—the woman
who has everything, who is everything
to him. Not that she knows
what would answer her need.
That's part of the guessing:
watching the face for a sign.

Meanwhile (as the Christmas story goes)
the Man who has everything to give
looks down upon his children.
Already he has granted
the work of his hands: the garden,
dimpled mountains, valleys, seven
glittering seas in which we splash.
What more? Maybe if he gives—
no he can't, that's too much,
too deep to dig, his own seed,
his heart's core. And such homely
wrappings: the belly of a girl
growing larger each day, how long
can she hold all she's been given,
pulled between the laws of God
and man, Mary the holy wishbone
breaking, but how else to bring forth
one who will split the world open
with his cries, and live divided,
one foot in heaven and one here below
where we breathe, sigh, stumble
our way down paths cobbled
from love and longing.

Not what we want,
the minister prayed last week,

but what we need. I bowed my head
and asked forgiveness for failing
to see the difference. Maybe it's the glare
of the season, maybe my husband
is right when he says *Lighting is everything.*
The whole world should be wired
to a dimmer switch. Too much light
is unkind, throwing shadows
like weapons across our lives,
showing up the threadbare places.
I bow my head and try again,
...my shepherd, I shall not want—
but I do, all of it, the world so finely
strung with lights and baubled,
and the pearls I hope are floating
on black velvet inside a box.

The movie has ended
and the children have fallen
heavily into dream like in holiday songs
where heads cloud with visions.
On the screen, credits are rolling,
names passing so quickly I can't read
them all, though I always try,
it's the least I can do, a nod
to those behind the scenes
who make miracles possible:
the boom operator, the make-up artist,
the caterer, the animal wrangler
who tries his hardest not to harm,
the gaffer, the Best Boy, Key Grip
and Dolly Grip and all the little Grips—
I think of them as a family, and maybe
they are, maybe they're all gathering

right now at the banquet table,
motioning for us to join them.
And who could refuse? Buttery oysters
are sliding from shells,
the sweet eclair is packed with cream,
and look, in the center,
the fatted suckling gleams.

All the Grandmothers of All the Poets
Show Up at a Reading

They've heard that their names will be bandied about,
their exploits swollen to inhuman proportions—black
matriarchs, Jewish bubbies, Catholic grandmothers bearing
rosaries, Norwegian grandmothers passing platters
of lutefisk and lefse. The room smells of talcum
and moth balls, dresses aired for the occasion, gardenia
sachets and cow pies, layer after layer of womanly sweat.
Some have come straight from the fields of the past, bent
like oxen over some mean task. One is up to her elbows in milk.
One is scrubbing her nails. My father's mother materializes
in the fuchsia dress she was buried in—even then,
she refused black. My mother's mother stuffs an apron
into the big brown pocketbook she accompanied for decades.
She doesn't understand the flimsy purses slung
over the poets' shoulders or strapped to their flat bellies.
A good pocketbook should last a lifetime.

A Pentecostal grandmother dead for years
lands with a whoosh on the front row. She's accustomed
to strange tongues; this is just one more
the audience keeps nodding to. Could that be Billy
up there at the podium, the one with the white beard?
The last time she saw him… but no, what yellow dog
is he talking about, and for sure she never slapped him.
Maybe that once, but why make a federal case out of it?
She keeps waiting to hear *love*, but he never says it plain.
Now he's on to the diary she kept meaning to burn.
Whispers begin at the back of the room, secrets
clicking, chain stitches, not a single one dropped

before it reaches her ear. She should have taken care
of things-—the letters and photographs. Well, he's done now,
and another taking his place, a slip of a thing
with eyes like burnt raisins: *My grandmother was a cave*,
she begins. An exhalation of wings from the balcony,
where those who have grown to myth and beyond
hover, fanning their powdered faces, relieved to be lost
among goddesses, cosmic eggs, hollow horns
of cornucopia, latticed honeycombs, their names
a mere mention at the front of some thin book: *In memory
of my grandmother. Rose Ellen. Beatrice. Marie.*

LAST WILL, ALMOST

It's that dream again
where I keep almost dying.
Heads are nodding,
they're reading a will
I don't recall signing.
What's left to leave
but saucers and books
and the thin gold ring
I keep in a box?
The nephews have gathered,
I'm the table spread
like in Psalm twenty-three.
I knot my spotted hands
across my chest, and try.

Behind closed eyes
I watch my name
roll off tomorrow's
presses, *predeceased by*—
then name after name,
as if death were a bus
I kept missing.
Black ink is collecting
into eyelids, jowls
that must be mine.
And there's another
old face, another,
a field of faces
to be skimmed over

like Sunday's identical
daisy-eyed brides.
My limbs grow heavy,
my breath backs up,
voices lull me, I'm almost gone
then startle awake!
a dead aunt's voice
rising from childhood's
petulant grave:
Ye shan't be missed,
her litany each time
I'd trundle off, yearning
to be begged back
as children do, having
nowhere to go, alone,

and one foot by one foot
is hard going, what if
no one waits at the other end,
no prince, no babies,
you might end up
like Auntie, dried apple
doll, cored and seeded,
caved-in smile. (When she died,
we barely paused, so tidily
she fit into the obit.)
If I shan't be missed,
I'll climb down and hide
under the table, a child

again, invisible,
powerful in absence:
Seeker come find me,
knock knock and I'll open.

Beneath the cloth
I'll wait till I glimpse
my parents' feet solid
in grown-up shoes,
not these dream feet
stuck in my view—
patent leathers, ruffled
socks turned down, sneakers
with dirt-caked soles,

and one pair of small
bare feet dangling:
she's too young yet
to touch the ground,
and why should she,
why hurry, there will be
plenty of time for that,
Mister Mud, Black Clay.
There's nowhere
I have to go just yet,
and no one else,
just yet, to be.

Writers' Conference, Last Dance

It writhes and bumps, grinds
    its hundred feet into the floor, antennae arms
        rising, one beast of flesh and musk breathing its single
          breath, this animal we make together larger

        than any of us alone—the young girl in haiku,
      her brief skirt banding a muscular rump
    (so much to say in such a small space),
the experimental novelist whispering

his many voices into the ear of the lyrical
    poet whose Ionic lines are breaking
        like waves around his neck while the journalist,
          invisible in the center of things, flings

        his arms into the air. In the corner an editor,
    all legs and black sheath, dances with herself,
  has been dancing like this all night, patiently
noting the scholar partnered by a cane.

Beneath trousers and dresses, old hamstrings strum,
    burn scars of envy tighten and recede, stockings
      web our spider veins, push-up forms lift us
        to a higher place or take the place

        of what's been taken. It's late, and we are not
    as we were when the dance began,
  or as my aunt once shouted, leaping in sprung
rhythm from her bed beside the dead

clock—*Oh my! It's later than it's ever been!*
    Last song, last frenzy of tentacles and centipedal
        fury, high heels skittering, sneakers squealing,
            the clomp of boots, the occasional bare foot

            risking it all as we fly momentarily
        up and out of ourselves—hurry, already
    we are splitting, already breaking apart in midair—
one pulse thumping, one heart beating fierce.

OPEN SWIM AT THE Y

Capped and goggled, I begin my crawl
with the other turtles at the shallow end.
Sometimes a winner crowns the waves,
like the muscled lifeguard who churns air to water,
water to air, in the perfect butterfly. But mostly
we are learners. Beside me, a hairless old man
recovers. *A stroke,* his wife whispers
as she dog-paddles to his pace. And at the edge
two retarded girls who call themselves Dumbo and Jumbo
are diving for pennies as if they were pearls.
Though shallow, it is a long way down for them,
with bodies like overgrown toddlers',
dragging the baggage of buttocks and breasts.
Through goggles I watch them underwater
the way I watched baby whales through the scratched
exhibit glass at Sea World when I was small
and believed all mongoloids were related, the same eyes,
slanted yet unbearably round. The same puffy face,
the same flesh collecting at the elbows and knees.
Now I am told not to call them mongoloids,
the world has renamed them, yet still the tribal name
floats to me and with it, a thirty-year memory—
how each morning as I waited alone at the stop,
their special bus would pass. Against the glass
they would press identical faces and smile,
waving their swollen hands as if to include me.
And I would turn from the love they gave so easily.
Now Jumbo taps my goggles, sticks a thumb in her ear,
wiggles her fingers. *Catch me!* she calls as she pulls
her sodden weight from the water, then, flat-footed,
slaps her way past the lifeguard. A woman dives in,

her false breast escapes and sails toward me
and I remember my aunt's mastectomy, the form
she tried so hard to fill. I rescue the breast and hand it back,
but she shrugs, tosses it onto her towel and kicks from me,
making her way. Rocked in her wake, Jumbo and Dumbo
bob past, twin buoys marking a safe passage. Dumbo turns
and waves, as if to seal some old contract, and I lift my hand,
turn my face to the water and begin my slow crawl back.

IV

THE ANGLE OF SHADOW, THE ANGLE OF LIGHT

Stand to one side. No, over here with me:
out of the light but out of darkness too...

—Richard Howard,
"Venetian Interior, 1889"

Demons

I beheld the Angel, who stretched out his arms,
embracing the flame of fire... This angel,
who is now become a devil, is my particular friend.
—William Blake, *The Marriage of Heaven and Hell*

One summer, even the air hurt
and sleep was just the sharp edge
I cut myself on each night.
My only nourishment, the small bone
of pain I chewed to the marrow.
Now I know why dogs hoard theirs.
Anything grows softer, sweeter,
if worked long enough. Outside
my window a church billboard:
The deeper you are hollowed out,
the more you can contain. I think
of the most beautiful woman I know
who wears a scar down the side
of her face. I think of bowls,
scooped out and hungry, and Job,
God's finest vessel. Blessed are
the meek, the persecuted, the poor
on whom the richest afflictions
are squandered. And those who wear
their wounds as a sign, like the whore
whose tears wet the dust on Christ's
feet while he rebuked the righteous:
He who is forgiven little, loves little.
The women at the shelter have been loved
almost to death—their raccoon eyes,
the blueprints of husbands on their arms,

their thighs. Friday nights the phones
ring off the hook, the men calling.
Sunday's bruises are healing, forgiveness
fills the air. And the women always answer.

We were poor, weren't we, Mother?
I ask, trying to rewrite my childhood.
Stretching those months in the Quonset hut
and erasing the four bedroom house.
Poverty: something I could have sunk
my teeth into. Happy art is the hardest to make.
Breughel's Tower of Babel is beautiful
and Blake's tygers of wrath
are wiser than his horses of instruction.

How silent the room of the boy's head
after the demons left—tables toppled,
empty chairs where they'd once sat,
arguing. No more late night plunges
into fire or water, no tussles
in afternoon grass. When Jesus called
Come Out! the little devils split,
and the boy was once again
his father's only child. At first
the crowd thought he was dead,
he was that still. Some said they heard
a cry issuing from the wound.

It has been three years since
that summer. I sleep the sleep
of the happily dead, wake singing
golden oldies, shop for potpourri
and wooden ducks, small things to make
the house a home. I'm smooth as a tray

or a rain gutter pointed downhill.
Convex, even, puffed up with joy
and health. Suffering could spill
over me and I wouldn't collect a drop.
I've joined the lonely procession
of the cured—the leper amazed at fingers
sprouting like leaves from the bark
of his arm, the old woman bent from birth,
who now walks like everyone else.
I think of the boy alone in his bed,
making room for the demons and trying
to dream them back. No wonder
after the transplant, the blind man
tried to scratch out his new eyes.
Suddenly, the bright world blinked
and blinked, until he learned what lids can do,
and pulled them down like shades,
and swam back to the darkness he knew.

His Place Or Yours?

A world of difference.
The space between

what might happen:

the dinner you serve in your mother's
hand-me-down apron, the dessert kiss
and its migratory ambition
to your bed with its chenille spread,
its hand-embroidered pillows

and what is planned:

the exact time (not four
but a quarter to) his dusty car pulling
into your driveway, the engine *humming*
listlessly beneath the hood. You wish
you could write *throbbing*,

it would let you both off the hook,

but you can't plead passion,
or the moon pulling
a *one night stand*. You remember waiting
by the screen door, wondering
why they always say *night*

when daylight offers equal opportunity.

And why *stand*, when circumstance

almost always lays us down.
One day lay, you decided, ashamed
but only for a moment. It was the first time
you were sure from the beginning

it was only for now.

The drive to his place
was several miles on a rutted road,
enough time to reconsider.
You weren't sure how to spell
his last name. He had not even bathed.

He smelled mothy as if his clothes

had been pulled from behind
some chair. You glanced sideways
at his profile, thinking of Michelangelo
studying the corpses in morgues,
cutting them apart to learn

how they worked. *The burden of stone*

he would later call the struggle
to resurrect what had been lost:
The way the marble stalled
against his chisel. The way centuries later
you scratch out a word too pretty

for what needs to be said,

and replace it with *trailer*,
what you knew even then

his place was: an aluminum can
on wheels. A room that was all bed,
not even a hook to secure your dress.

The tinny sound of the door
shutting, its insubstantial echo.

After Reading That "Pathology" and "Poetry" Share the Same Root

Twin sisters, each hiding
beneath her cloak
scars that keep
lovers returning,
the way we can't forget
bad girls who tumble
the happy ending on its head.
*And who played the ingenue,
what was her name?*

Carcinoma, name me.
Thrombus, strum
your music, tune me
to a deeper key, rhyme me
with something, anything—
lyre lyre life on fire
in the tender place
the passion-doctor
enters. Stitches,
if you must heal, leave
a fine white scrabble,
seam to follow.

ELEMENTAL

Since the affair, my husband's hands
have prophesied leaks, forestalling a future
of torn gutters, vents. Every month

a new filter strains the air
through fine nets. He is astounded
at what accumulates. *Dust!* he cries.

I add, *Time.* For years a framed collage
of sand and glass has hung at our window,
staining the bed and our faces

with chunks of cathedral light—amber,
turquoise, red. Last night the frame
began pulling away. *It's just a matter*

of time, he said. *And gravity*, I whispered,
stepping out to a world that spins
on habit and trust. When I returned,

he was kneeling in sand
and splintered wood, the chisel a sharp
failure beside him. Relics of glass,

broken and beautiful, scattered
the light between us. I took his hands
and brought them to my face.

Never, Ever

What I thought
I could never forgive
now salts the mustached
edge of his lip

Not the act   I will never…

But his hunger

for a mouth new
as a wife's
can never be

a mouth (I later learned
begging for details)
tinged with the taste
of tobacco and Scotch

Oh to be the bad
woman for someone

How good I would taste

And the buzz

he must have felt
the insect whirring
in his brain   the approach
of wings   the landing

*

But it was worth it
wasn't it my friend asks

I mean now that you're
back together and better

She says it the way
the sighted make heroes
of the blind   the way
we believe amputees
grow suddenly noble

She says it
in a hungry way like she really
needs to know

                              the taste   the buzz

my friend whose husband
would never   Could
never

The Husbands of Poets

They think we love them
for their connections, and we let them
think it. Gail's husband, skilled in modem
and fax, labors to hook her up to the world,
and Walt built a walkway for Melanie,
a winding path between studio and house.
Even Suzanne, long divorced, keeps
a *husband* on her bed, a big-armed pillow
made of durable material. She sprawls against it
as she writes, pounds its chest when in need
of lumpy comfort. To love a man
is to be caught between a rock and a soft place.
At Diana's book party, her husband's face
crumpled into his hands, then lifted, shining:
I stand reflected in her light.

My husband calls it poetic injustice,
what we do to them. He doesn't know the half
of it. How we steal their dead mothers
and lovers for the heart knowledge,
listening in bed for the dreams they release,
feral, untranslatable. But already
we are translating. Already we are at our desks,
holding their lives like globes of fruit,
turning them over, expectant.

The Other Woman

In dreams I always love her.
We sit shaded
beneath big hats,
sipping mint tea, laughing.
I admire the flame
of her hair, the delicate
freckled wrist.

We ask small questions:
Did he always fold his towel
just so, over the banister?
Do Wednesdays still
knit his brow?
Her pale stockings
rub together.
Her voice, torn lace.

Across our faces
sun weaves
a lattice of
shadow and light.
We sit shaded
beneath big hats,
asking small questions,
nodding.

Ancient Weaving: the Mistress to the Wife

Each evening I knit him back to you.
As long as I am here, he will never
forget the way home. You dream yourself

Penelope, me the island woman, but see
how the years unravel in my hands
as he tells me the story, recalling

the long-ago curve of your neck
beneath the lamp, the child
woven into the fold of your arm.

I nod in his direction, my fingers
on the photograph he shows:
you in the kitchen, bending to carve

the meat, lean and rare as the body
you believe I serve him. But come closer,
watch as he opens my robe and it falls

to the floor and my breasts, powdered,
heavy as yours, catch in the net
of his hands as they move to my thighs,

an old story he reads, remembering
you, me, the ancient seam
of what you most fear,

of what you are sure must be satin
and dark. If you look
it will stun you: the bed's whiteness,

the wind-fresh cotton I've folded
with hands like a mother's
that stroke him, counting each leap

of his pulse until I sleep
and dream I curl in the rim of the saucer
that holds the teacup you cradle each night.

Trying to Escape Autobiography

For the nine-year-old girl in the poetry class
who titled her poem "The truth is sticky."

You would slide to a bluer place
or colorless. Write a cloud poem
mothers read rocking away evenings.
Boneless as cats dreaming or faceless
pictures a child connects
dot-to-dot in his mind.

But truth glues itself to the back
of your eyes. Just when you thought
you'd wiped the table clean, your elbow
catches in a smear of it.

This is the clasp and leech of real.
Mucilage. The daily molasses.
And *who has dipped my wings in syrup*
while I slept? asked the moth, breathless.

You want those made-up people.
But they limp your cousin's limp.
Every scent your mother's. Each breath
your father's last wheeze.
Bones clank through your poems,
their marrow sticky, dripping.

The Angle of Shadow, The Angle of Light

The hall where they are kept is a broken
wing off the main building, and in the last desk
a boy named Achilles is back
from a battle with the school psychologist,
who put him in Time Out for pissing
in a sink and beating his head
against a chalkboard until it bled.
I am the visiting poet. This is the class
of special students I have been warned against.
Last night I read an artist's notebook:
The angle of shadow must be equal
to the angle of light, so this morning
in my bag of kaleidoscopes and prisms
and peacock feathers, I packed a hard black
stone and the sun-bleached skull of a cow.

Achilles: his name tag is my cue. *A hero*
from a famous book, I say. *The greatest*
warrior of all. But the boy is shaking
his head, he's heard this before
and is ready with a sneer—*My name's*
from a cartoon. Later in the teachers' lounge
I learn he has been dipped in the river
more than once. His mother is gone,
he has gonorrhea of the mouth from his father,
and now when he draws a self-portrait
he sketches in fangs and fur
on the palms of his hands. *When I touch him*
he flinches, the teacher says.

The first Achilles had a caretaker, a centaur
who fed him lion entrails and the marrow
bones of bears to give him courage,
but what can I give this boy?
If words were enough,
I would trace them on bread and offer
a bite. Or like the ancient mystic,
outline them in sand, and we would
lick up the ones that would save us.

I want to believe what the Greeks believed,
that in the beginning, the unbroken
dark, a tiny seed slumbered
and when Night coupled with Death
she hatched an egg and named it Light.
It is said that in the midst of battle
the sun blazed from Achilles' head
and his shout was brighter than trumpets.
But finally nothing could save him.
Not the shield fashioned by Hephaestus,
the greaves and helmet forged
in darkness and laid at Achilles' feet.
Not even the cry that reached
his mother, lost in the caves
of the sea and immortally helpless.

NOT HERE

Emerging from the tunnel edging the park
        and into the searing light, a boy
carrying on his shoulders a black garbage bag
        as though it contained his life,

and behind him a man, carrying only
        himself, his body stooped, feet shuffling
in shoes meant for a larger man. His eyes are sad
        the way an animal's eyes are sad,

raw sense unrelieved by understanding.
        The two are together and I am walking
with my husband on an autumn Sunday
        so brilliant you'd gladly pay

if the universe were charging:
        all that's missing is a child.
Which may be why I look towards the boy
        when the man comes at him,

and must be reminded by my husband
        who is wiser in matters like these:
You can't change their lives, let it go.
        The man lunges for the boy and begins

to strike, and the boy leans into the pain,
        pleading *Not here!* as if there were
some better place for this to happen. Now
        the boy is up, circling the man, goading him,

teasing, as if this were his part to play,
        no choice in the casting or in the lines
some hand has written, which he delivers to the man:
        you goddamn son of a bitch get away from me,

do I have to bite you again? The man comes at him
        again and the boy drops to his knees, his hands
shielding his face. The black bag has opened,
        spilling its contents onto the burnished leaves,

and the boy begins, reverently,
        to gather in his arms the trousers
and socks, the sweaters and cups, a few papers
        which he stuffs into the bag, glancing

up, and again up, so as not to lose sight
        of the man disappearing into the trees.
You fuckin' asshole wait up, he cries,
        don't leave me here alone.

Invocation

Even Christ at the end called out in holy terror,
Let this cup (the sky is silent)
then looked to his right and left, grateful
for any company, thief or murderer.
Forgive them for they know (a shadow passes over).

*

A girl on a table, splayed
between strangers. Cold instruments
clamping, a nurse squeezing her hand.
She might have cried *Son* or *Daughter,*
knowing not what she did, but all that came
from her mouth was *Mother,* the rest
rushing nameless into the waiting basin.

*

The kamikaze whose name was never called
tells it to the camera: *We were trained
to cry out to the emperor at the end.
I thought I might call* Father, *but it is hard
to cry* Father *when you are dying.
I remembered a geisha I had loved,
thinking when the time came
I would call her name,* Misaka.

*

When the old man in his last moment surfaced
from the morphine, calling *Mom*
like some fevered child, his daughter
rose from the cot and stumbled toward him.

*

A long-ago lover once made me swear
I would hurry to him in his last hour,
no matter where or when.
His name is lost, but not the press
of his arm pulling me toward the promise,
insisting *There's nobody else.*

*

My dying aunt called simply *Somebody*—
and a janitor sweeping the corridor
outside her room, answered.

COMMUNION

The old man, having lost so much and moving
each day closer to the first infancy,
stirs on the couch where I have propped
his body and spirit, mind having fled
long ago to some corner of the swept room
or out the window where a woman
he no longer knows clips to a line
white things the wind is trying to rob her of.
Did you take a nap? I ask. He shakes his head:
Nowhere to take it from, and I nod at the mad
wisdom of what is left, hollow dipper,
scooped-out ladle fearful of lowering itself
into the well that serves up death as easily as rest.
Then, as if he cannot lose one more thing
and still remain, he wipes from his eye
a crumb of sleep and puts it to his mouth.

Traveling

When the Egyptians packed their dead,
the brain was first to go, pulled
with tweezers through the nose.
Then a slit in the side and the rest
poured out, the soft parts they tamped
separately into Canopic jars
or simply bandaged and stuffed back in
like giblets I rummage from the cavity
of the baking hen and present
to my cat, who slurps the juicy heart
and in this I stray one step
from the Egyptians, who kept
the heart intact for the crossing
to the land of the dead, where
it would be weighed in the balance
pan, opposite Truth which was a feather.
And any heart that tipped the scales
was eaten by Amemait the Devourer.

My husband refuses to sign the line
giving it all up. *Call it my last
selfish act,* he says, *but I'm keeping
my goddamn eyes.* I'm a card-carrying donor.
I've checked the blanks: Eyes. Kidneys.
Liver. Spleen. I'm holding off on the heart.
If I die this morning, by noon my parts
will be floating, not in Canopic urns,
but more like the Mason jars lining the cellar,
beets and cucumbers swimming in brine.

You can't take it with you, but we try,
like the old woman in the news.
It's my whole life, she cried
as the tractor ripped through her home,
shoveling tons of garbage, seven refrigerators,
clothes, rotting food three feet high.
The excavation crew wore masks
to escape the air she slept in.

My grandmother swept up after herself
leaving nothing but a line
of grandchildren and one string of advice:
*Travel light. Take only what you can't
live without.* When Grandpa died,
she had nineteen dollars. She bought
a bus ticket and packed a suitcase,
one dress for each season.
On my overseas trip, I carried
bread and cheese and one small suitcase
filled with all the wrong things,
nothing fit for the weather.
The mummy I saw was Cleopatra,
age eleven, daughter of Candace,
who took with her a wooden comb,
a string of berries, a floral leaf.
Something for vanity, something for hunger,
something for memory's sake.
When my aunt died, we picked through
the rubble. Bundles of birthday cards,
widowed buttons, scarves, napkins pressed
flat in the backs of drawers.
Finally it took a bonfire.
And the things we couldn't live without
fit easily into a hamper.

Enough

Once I cupped my hand like a beggar's
and poked it in God's face.
Give, Give! I cried, counting
on my fingers the meager riches left.

*

Pocketless we slide into this world
and pocketless we shall return,
the scripture says, or something.
Where then to store the rest: Eve's apple,
the crust of unleavened bread, the coin
newly minted, itchy in our hand?
Sew a pouch, a purse, stitch a valise, secure
the filled hamper between
the camel's humps, cinch the saddlebag,
the suitcase, and here's a key
for the steamer trunk, the vault, the safety deposit box,
the attic and basement, the self-storage units
where we store our selves. Look out the window:
even the can man gleaning the returnables
has trouble lifting the load.

*

Who could have foreseen such wind-blown
prosperity: the seed effortlessly
breaking its husk, sunshine of biblical proportions,
and sufficient unto the day the rain thereof.
Okay, I said. *If it's that or nothing,*

and opened my hands to whatever
heaven might throw down.

*

Peel back the bark of desire,
says the priest of less. *Uncover bare need:*
roof over your head, an apple a day.
But what of night, opening like a blossom?
And the wisteria, grape-heavy,
ornamental, its many-clustered shadow
against a neighbor's house. Give us
this day. Forgive us this day.

*

Enough, cries the river spilling its banks,
the mountain worn down to stone,
the cloud having swallowed its fill of sky,
the lidded teapot, steaming.

TWIG

Snapped branch
    from which no fruit dangles

maidens   bachelors   stillbirths
    snipped vas deferens
tubes of Fallopia

    seeds scattered   blown:

the uncle who married a woman who would not yield
    the nephew who cared only for boys
        the sister who loved the husbands of other women
    the cousin whose belly bloated falsely each month

the aunt whose single hope knotted like a cyst
    (over her bed a framed weaving:
    the braided hair of grandmothers and great-

    blonde   mahogany   chestnut)

*

Roots of ancient trees:
    I've seen them split sidewalks   rise like bones
      of a behemoth buried shallow   extinct before its time

In the vast green land of genealogy
    the roots spread thick above my head
I dangle   between father and mother
    no progeny   only two consecutive husbands
who always looked before they leapt

whose ledgers always balanced
so why take on…

(each week I check the cartons
for broken yolks before I buy)

*

A dying man places an ad   *Needed:*
    someone to go in, half, on a family plot

and my friend an aging homosexual
calls me *daughter*

*

After my sister pushed out her last son
    I cut the blue ribbon
and the doctor tied my nephew like a gift

Days later when the remnant dropped onto the changing table
    I picked it up:
        black stub   charred knob

Mother Father   hear how they roll off the tongue like   *river forever*

Aunt snaps
tight like a locket

Not James

The man who used to drive me to the train
is dead. I did not know him well.
Around the writers' table he kept a proper
distance: collar pressed, manicured
stories of gardens and dogs. "Your humble student,"
he would quip, and when the hour's clock
ran out, "Your chauffeur awaits."
"Home, James," I would answer, though James
was not his name. His car smelled newer
than it was, a few graying dog hairs
on the seat, the only clue to a fiercer life.
He loved mystery books, his recently
buried wife, the ghost of his doting mother,
an only-childhood in the groves
of California—a green recollection we shared,
along with cloverleaf freeways on which
we both were raised. Oh yes, he would nod,
he too remembered moonlit rumors
of grunion runs, wave after wave spawning
thousands of silver fishes that wriggled
their eggs into the sand, then were gone.
Like me, he waited on the beach, fruitlessly,
for years. Like me, he was childless.
None to inherit his car, his dogs, the box
of stories from which he read lightly
each week, though once or twice a crack
of darkness peeked through. The week
before he died he sent a list of mysteries
I should read, I who always tangle in details
before the end is solved. The paper reported
he was found sitting in his car, the dog

beside him freshly walked. It mentioned
a fiancée somewhere, of which he had never
spoken. "Gentle reader," he would have called you,
this man who used to drive me to the train.

The Invention of Zero

All along we knew something   was missing   We had no idea
it was nothing   We knew only that we lacked
a place to place   the sum of our subtractions

The ancient woman who buried her children   one by one
ticking off their deaths on her fingers   lost count
when the last one was gone   could only rattle her fist

at the unbroken sky   and the man beside her
had no way to factor   the absolute   chill growing inside him
Then one day a dream bubble   round and filled

with emptiness   floated and popped   in the head
of a unknown Babylonian   who woke no less a man
and no more   for having slept with   Zero

In the sand he drew the shape   of nothing
and we circled the miracle   our counting sticks collapsing
beside us   and bowed to the power of   Zero

Origin   Original   Indivisible   Irreducible
Wholly itself   Wholly   nothing   all things being equal
and they are   all the great and countable things   unaccountable

without Zero   The man drowning in pennies   swimming
in pennies that might have buried him   without making him
one thin dime   the man they now call a millionaire   no more than

a million air bubbles   rising from the inflatable chest   of Zero
bottom dweller   who loves the view   somewhere between plus
and minus   yes and no   lolling happily in its shapeless shape

Zero   dipping a wand in the bottle   blowing something
from nothing   releasing a cartoon balloon   that breaks
on the surface   Don't forget where you came from

then birthing a garland of zeros   string of pearls bobbing
beside the first penny the man ever held   Our lives bulge
with the power of Zero   dollars snub dimes   dimes leave pennies

lying in the gutter   How easily we forget   what has made us
what can break us   Zero smiles   rolls over
expels another round   and a woman in a diner somewhere

flutters a lottery ticket before her boss's eyes   unties
her apron   and is gone   to nowhere in particular
Anything times Zero erases itself   and it's all the same

to Zero   expandable halo   lasso   noose
asking nothing of us   taking nothing from us
cannot divide us   can only multiply   all our somethings

into nothing   rock us   the last lost child
of the empty-fisted woman   uncounted   unaccountable
rock us in armless arms   back to where we came from

V

DEEP LIGHT

In a dark time, the eye begins to see.

—Theodore Roethke,
"In a Dark Time"

INTERVAL

Once my mother, dressing
for an obligation, stepped
through the moment
into my eyes, half-finished,
a woman in a black dress.
All that she would momentarily
add up to, strewn across the bed—
satin gloves, a beaded bag,
the seed pearls chattering.
Fill, we say, when we speak
of life and power. *The room
filled with her presence.
Her voice filled the room.*
Yet my mother emptied
so beautifully the room—
her black dress, pure light
distilled to its essence.
In the corner a record
was playing and I heard
for the first time
the spaces between—
the guitarist's fingers
worrying the frets. The intake
of breath before the singer
launched the waiting song.

Her Nakedness

At the market I see a beautiful woman—
her gray hair long and untamed, her only adornment
a three-tiered necklace of lines. The skin
on her hands is dappled with sun spots,
and her voice opening on *hello* is ripe,
slightly bruised at the edges like the peaches
she places in a basket. She moves slowly
through the aisles, considering what not to buy.
I follow closely, pushing my loaded cart
and trying to imagine needing so little, year by year
learning what to step out of. First, these high heels,
rickety stairs on which I topple. I'll exchange them
for cushioned oxfords that breathe something back,
or open sandals like the ones the beautiful woman wears.
At home, I unpeel my stockings and slide
into soft shoes, lift my long skirt
high to the mirror, practicing how it will be
when I earn enough courage. Twice this summer
I've flaunted my purple veins to people I hardly know.
I don't want to become the woman in the story
who bathed in rubber underwear, ashamed for God
to see her nakedness. *Her Nakedness,* so royal a title
for such a bald sight. My aunt, who lost
her thick black hair, wears a wig for strangers.
But at home, holding court beside a new husband
and a niece with a full crown of hair, she removes
the wig and stares into our eyes, as if daring us to love her.

THE ROUND EARTH'S IMAGINED CORNERS

Here in this retirement village the earth
takes its sweet time spinning.
It's summer, after all, and California.
My friend greets me at the entrance, holding keys
inherited from a daughterless old man
she cared for and finally loved. We pass
beneath a gargantuan globe, a bulging corset
of longitude and latitude on which are floating
seven blue seas and seven green continents
reaching out with isthmian fingers as if longing
to touch one another. In my mind
is an African proverb: *I am poor*
and I will die. You are rich and you will die.
Yards are littered with blossom—hydrangea,
hibiscus, the lethal oleander. At our feet, alyssum
and baby's tears, and stretching as far as we can see,
mass plantings of patios, terraces, chalets, villas
like the one where the old man lived out his days,
his body light in my friend's arms, bones hollow
and angled as wings. All day his wheelchair
circled the crowded rooms, navigating
Italian sculpture, French brocade, crystal that sings
with a flick of a finger, first editions of Milton
and Donne—*at the round earth's imagined*
corners, blow your trumpets, angels.

A woman waves from the doorway
of a garden home. A fig tree arches above her.
We are walking Via Mariposa, named
for what flutters one summer, at most,
and is gone. The avenue's perpetual curve

suggests one route looping this green place,
but I'm not sure until we meet twice, three times,
the same biker sailing the same hill toward us.
Like Magellan we discover the new world
through its repetitions, the past emerging
inch by inch over the horizon: helmet, reflective
vest, spokes and wheels revolving. The house,
the dog, our mother's hat, someone dying
in someone's arms. Oh yes, we've seen
that ship before, that same old sun.

THERE ARE DAYS

There are days when nothing
especially goes right but nothing
wrong, and you find yourself
writing to your sister-in-law
to thank her for the lemon cake
she baked that time, and for loving
your brother all these years.
Three, maybe four times that day
you praise whoever is responsible
for letting you pee so easily,
without pain, without the tubes
and bags your uncle rolled on a cart
beside him that last year. You dig
in the garden until sweat pearls
your lip and you taste the salt
you have made, remembering the poem
a small girl wrote after her father was shot:
I love myself because I am not dead.
In bed that night you spread your toes.
The furnace of your brain warms
the pillow, the heart's engine ticks,
and the lungs, those meaty wings,
flutter and empty, flutter
and empty, lifting you into sleep.

Easter Monday, Central Park

The clouds are putting on airs this morning, my earphones
    tuned to Grieg, between public radio's appeals
        to give what I can. On every walkway, April's profusion

of nannies, skaters, butterflies, dogs. And the homeless—
    who aren't, exactly, having made their home
        quite soundly here, like this couple stretched out full

in Sheep Meadow, her head on his shoulder, his hat
    open on his chest as if expecting contributions to drop
        from a large distance. Nearby, a soft man sprawls

beneath a pergola where wisteria droop grapelike
    above him, their thick vines twisted into the beauty
        van Gogh taught us to see. Beautiful, too, on closer inspection,

are these bumblebees large as thumbs, droning
    their static. Each one a queen, winter's surviving
        colonist carrying the future inside her. Now sliding

towards me, a sleek carriage is steered by a Japanese mother
    and I'm thinking *money* and *time on her hands*,
        her child some Suzuki violin tuned to early perfection–but no,

as they pass I see a body gnarled by fate, thin legs filed
    to toe-less points, head lolling like a rain-heavy flower
        on narrow stem. The mother strokes his face with a petal hand

and it's Grieg again in my ears, his "Wand of Youth"
    conducting a row of old women on the lawn, morning stretches
        led by a black leotard. Seated, they are ballerinas-of-the-folding-

chair, their pale arms reaching, waving. Pollen sifts
  onto their shoulders, and at my feet purple thrift sprouts
    beside a dead tree someone has found a use for, sawed it off

at a sturdy juncture and hammered a birdhouse
  where sparrows feed. We make do, use what is given.
    Last month after a surprise storm and every slope filling

with families and red toboggans, I watched
  two sled-less boys laugh themselves to the top
    of a hill, and when their turn came, one laid himself

belly down on the snow, the other climbed
  onto his friend's back, and together they slid,
    yelping joy, to the bottom of the hill, where they stood,

brushed themselves off and hurried
  to the top again, Boy-Sled's chance now to become Boy,
    to steer his friend's body safely down.

TRIBE

The morning we buried his brother, my father
sat beside the grave on a folding chair
among his siblings, a scoop of Illinois dirt
readied for the ritual fling. My mother and I
and assorted others once or twice
removed by generation or marriage
kept our careful distance behind the row
reserved for family, which seemed to mean
two brothers and a string of white-haired
sisters gathered to lay their younger brother
down. I held my mother's arm, the narrow
heels of our Sunday pumps sinking into earth
softened from weeks of June rain, the kind of rain
farmers like my grandfather prayed for,
but that was decades gone, before
this band of children grew into husbands, wives,
grandparents and great-, before the dimming
of their radiant hair, when their lives carried
only the burden of *sister, brother*. A clan
with look-alike eyes, who stood in line
for Saturday's scrub in the metal tub,
who steered the blinkered mule
down and up the soybean plot. Then on
to school where they coveted the fruit
in the town children's buckets. From first light
to lantern, their world was disc and harrow,
barter and sell, the huckster wagon,
the egg woman and the cream man
and for joy a black pony named Betty
that the boys quickly outgrew.

*

After the casseroles in the church basement
and dizzy from lilies I climbed
into the back of my parents' car
and watched my father unhitch his tie
and kiss his sisters, and place himself
upright in the driver's seat. *Little brother,*
he said quietly to the air, then took the key
from his pocket. For hours it seemed
gravity locked us, the only movement my parents'
heads swiveling and nodding as if on stalks
while the striped world of soybean
and dirt—green, black, green, black—
flickered past the silence
that I too held, thinking of my uncle,
whose medical gift of eyes and marrow
might even now be waking
in some stranger's body, a child perhaps,
or woman: how do such things go?
Across the state line, rain clouds broke
and a farmhouse appeared, looped
by a white fence beside which a boy
on a tiny motorcycle patrolled the scene.
Look! I said. My father slowed the car.
Had this been a movie, I would have rubbed
my eyes. *Every child should have a place like that,*
my mother said, pointing to the field
where the herd of miniature horses
I thought I had imagined, grazed.
Real as a dream, or the song
from my own lost days: *dapples and grays.*
I rolled down the window and waved
to the boy, who did not look up. No grownup
in sight, no scale against which to measure
his task, this world that seemed all to him.

The Tellable

Praise the world to the Angel, not the untellable...
Tell him things. He'll stand more astonished.
— Rainer Maria Rilke, *The Duino Elegies*

I had it wrong: your need, not mine,
that Saturday morning you found me
dirt-crusted in the garden. Thinking it mattered,
I bowed my head, but you were engaged
elsewhere, tracing patterns the black earth
had planted on my bare feet. I watched as from your wings
the lost ones unfolded—the dead sister, grandmothers
and grandfathers, the child that might yet be,
all I ever loved or one day will
sifted like pollen as you shook out your feathers.
Had you been less, had I not been so sure
your visit was on my account,
I might have stilled for a moment, heard
your bird heart thumping out its hunger.

If you come back, I promise to show
what you came to see—my dusty shelves, things
upon things, the smudged prints on all
I touch. This is my parents' wedding picture. Look,
my father had all his fingers then, before he lost one
to the fan belt the year I was born.
He is still alive on this earth, which I count
a miracle, but miracles are not what you came for.
Here is a tarnished frame (time blackens silver)
and a picture of the youngest nephew.
When I hold him, I smell apricot
pablum, rubber pacifier, the scent of recent

wind on his jacket—he always carries the outside
in. This is my piano, with its eighty-eight keys.
We live with limits, E-flat above middle-C
is my favorite. The wren on the mantle is stone,
a gift from a friend who is tall as humans go,
long-limbed with graceful bones.
The egg in its nest is real, it dropped from a tree
last April; gravity is another limitation.
By the window is my middle-aged
cat with his slack belly. We age, we loosen,
my jowls are yielding, my husband's hips
broadening, he is learning to cry.
This is the watercolor of a stream my aunt painted
after her husband died. The ones who leave,
we try to paint them back, write them back.
But you see the lost ones all the time,
that's not why you came. Here, dip your wing
in the stream, watch the water shiver.

My Father's Cadillac

While other men flipped
through *Playboy*, their eyes
fixed on the creased beauties,
my father fingered the slick
pages of new car catalogs, stood outside
the transparent walls of showrooms
as the objects of his desire spun
on the turntable decade after decade,
cars he kept denying himself
for the line of boxy sedans
and station wagons solid enough
to hold six children, who soon dispersed
to the convoy of used Bugs and Beetles
filling our driveway like an army
of hard-shelled insects, each haggled
at a discount from some widow or retiree,
each housing in its driver's seat
a teenager whose only desire was to peel
away, a father's love
bright as headlights in our eyes.
It took thirty years and the slicing
of his chest, a plastic valve
set like an odometer to empty itself
after five years, tops,
for my father to finally say yes
to this Cadillac where we sink
into blue leather. The control panel
beams Good Morning, All Systems Go.
Enjoy your inheritance, my father says.
You're riding in it. We laugh

about the man who was buried in his car.
My father asks if I remember
the photograph of *his* father standing
before that '57 Chevy—his last car, his last
trip out west. All I recall is a big white
house of a car framing a man bent with age
and emphysema, his eyes squinting
against the California sun. The climate
in the Cadillac is a year-round seventy.
We could be anywhere, we could be
in the air, sailing, or coasting
on a blue ship toward some white-sand
miracle, like this place we've arrived
years after the warranty on my father
has run out. *Ninety-six thousand miles
on this baby*, he says, caressing the padded
dashboard. The cruise control is set,
the spring-loaded coils beneath us poised
to absorb shock from within or without.
Ninety-six thousand miles, and still she shines.

TEACHING A NEPHEW TO TYPE

Because you lag already
years behind the computer-and-
otherwise-literate boys with fathers,
and your handwriting is a tangle
the teachers have grown weary
of unraveling, and because you are as close
to a son as I can manage, though nothing
about you is manageable anymore,

I am teaching you to type. The trick
is to look anywhere but down.
Your fingers are dumb birds pecking,
just follow the chart I've made.
We'll begin in the thick of things,
the home row to which we'll always
return. Little finger on *a*. Then tap
your way next door to *s*. Now

you've made *as*. Don't think, I say.
Just watch the chart: *dad   sad   fad*
a flash   a flask   a lad had.   Tomorrow
we'll move on to reach and return
and the period key, but for now
just use the comma, it's like catching
a breath, or you can type a colon,
double dot, old snake eyes, luck
in your future, meaning *watch this space:*
something is about to follow.

News

for a sister

It is March, mud weather,
and the worms have left signatures,
castings of their former selves.
Your sons are outside turning
over rocks, searching the chaos
of kingdom and phylum for some
small order—a slug or centipede
bristling with life. I join them,
eager to trace in this changing
calligraphy some further mention
of spring. Yesterday the cancer
tests came back and tomorrow
the sac that grew these children
will be clamped and pulled out.
And you will lie in white forgetfulness
while the pathologist reads your cells'
possible futures. But in this moment
you are here, sweeping the porch.
Helicopter leaves circle your head,
husks carried by the wind.
The younger son shovels a universe
of soil into a bucket while the eldest
smears dirt across his temple,
a primitive marking. Below our feet
whole worlds go on without us
and everything tapers down to a dark
burrowing, like the common worm,
Lumbricus terrestris, who makes its way
by swallowing the earth which is

its chief obstacle. Inch by blind inch
it thrusts its blunt head forward,
pulsing with blood and carrying
more hearts than it will ever use.

First Husband

After the marriage exploded, it sifted
down to this: the scar your fist left
on the filing cabinet where I kept my poems,
and on the ironing board stacks of Army khakis
whose pleats never flattened to your satisfaction.
It helped to think of you that way, a detonation
searing my eyes from everything but the white flash
that lit my path years later to a place
where I was still young enough to pass
as a bride. I've kept you hidden, even my friends
don't know. And I had almost buried you
when the Christmas card came—your fourth wedding,
complete with children acquired along the way.
Your chest has dropped, and gone completely
is the hairline that began its early retreat
when you were still the boy I would marry.
Your shirt is wrinkled; beside you
the new wife is already starting to fade.
Something in her chin reminds me of me. I send
my best wishes. For finally after twenty years
a memory ripens and falls into my lap:
our last trip, a Canadian forest
where strange animals destined for extinction
roamed the green hills. At a roadside stand,
we stopped for melons. Later, you steered
with one hand, and all the way down the mountain
I licked the sweetness from your fingers.

First Meeting After the Separation

Where else could it have been
but here in the dark

where theatre seats
assure a plush distance,

your hand bordering
the armrest. And what other movie

but this one—wordless, animal—
the silence between us labored

as the bear's breathing.
His companion dead, he makes

a bed in her fur, slowing
his heart for the long sleep

in which the bone of survival
hardens and he begins

the journey back.
Out of winter, past spring

and into the thickening
summer I trail him,

imagining a snake's coil
and rattle, a hunter

crouching in ambush.
Be careful, I whisper,

as if the bear could hear,
as if anything could turn him

from the honeyed air,
his body loping

across territories of thorn
and mountain, over the next

blind pass, and the next,
carrying all that hunger.

To the Absent Wife of the Beautiful Poet
at the Writers' Conference

I want you to know that nothing happened,
and everything that might have is now sewn
into the hoop of Arizona sky
that stretched above our heads that shy
evening of talk when we left our books
and went out to read the papery news
of bougainvillea. Here was vegetation
more animal than plant, the dangerous spine
of cactus, its fleshy stem and thistle,
and those rubbery tongues lolling speechless
in the desert air where even domestic
herbs turn wild, parsley and dill spilling
over their planned containers. When your husband
broke off a piece of rosemary and held it
out to me, I smelled the sharp clean scent
of marriage, the scent that fills my loved world
three time zones away. My garden, the spotted
cat and aged brandy, the bed pillow minted
with the imprint of my husband's head.
Yet I confess that part of me wanted
to take in that moment the man you more
than half-made, knowing that what I love
most in married men is what is given
by wives. The elbow he leans upon
is *your* elbow, his listening quiet,
your quiet, practiced in twenty years
of bedtime conversation. If he loved,
in that instant, anything in me, it was
the shape and smell of one whole woman
made from the better halves of two—

your hard earned past and my present, briefly
flaming. Not long ago I watched a girl
I might have been twenty years ago, sit
literally at my husband's feet and adore him.
There are gifts we can give our husbands,
but adoration is not one. If I could,
I would be one woman diverging, walk
one road toward those things that matter
always, the trail long love requires.
The other, for what burned in the eyes
of your husband as he asked, *What is the secret
to a long marriage?* I gave my grandfather's
bald reply: *You don't leave and you don't die.*
There are no secrets. Together, the four of us—
your husband, mine, you and I,
have lasted. I started to say forty
married years, but no, it is eighty,
each of us living those years sometimes,
by necessity, singly, the whole of love
greater than the sum of its combined hearts.
That's what I mean about the sky. Its blueness
and the way it goes on forever. An old
teacher told me if you break a line in half
again and again, you will never reach an end.
Infinity is measured by the broken spaces
within as well as by the line spooling out
as far as we can see. I love my husband.
Still, there were spaces in that evening
that will go on dividing our lives. And if
the sky had not begun in that moment
to blink messages of light from stars I thought
had died out long ago, I might have answered
your husband's eyes another way.
And there would have been heaven to pay.

Making Love

Why *make?* I used to wonder.
Is it something you have to keep on
making, like beds or dinner, stir it up

or smooth it down? Sex, I understood,
an easy creaking on the upholstered
springs of a man you meet in passing.

You *have* sex, you don't have to make it,
it makes *you*—rise and fall and rise again,
each time, each man, new. But love?

It could be the name of a faraway
city, end of a tired journey you take
with some husband, your bodies chugging

their way up the mountain, glimpsing
the city lights and thinking, If we can
keep it up, we'll make Love by morning.

I guess it was fun for somebody,
my grandmother once said. By then
I was safely married and had earned

the right to ask, there in the kitchen
beside the nodding aunts. Her answer
made me sad. In her time, love meant making

babies, and if I had borne twelve
and buried three, I might see my husband
as a gun shooting off inside me, each bullet

another year gone. But sex wasn't my question.
Love was the ghost whose shape kept
shifting. For us, it did not mean babies,

those plump incarnations the minister
had promised—flesh of our flesh,
our *increase*. Without them, and twenty years

gone, what have we to show
for the planing and hammering, bone
against bone, chisel and wedge,

the tedious sanding of night
into morning—when we rise, stretch,
shake out the years, lean back,

and see what we've made: no ghost,
it's a house. Sunlight through the window
glazing our faces, patina of dust

on our arms. At every axis, mortise
and tenon couple and hold. Doors
swing heavy on their hinges.

Fortune

In the land of married
takeout and delivery, what is meant for one
sometimes feeds two. Which means

one cookie, scented with almond,
that we break in common,
pulling our fortune from its shell.

Once we broke our life open to find:
nothing, which shouldn't have surprised.
One plus one sometimes equals

one plus one, all those dark months
together. How many shared
dinners since then, impossible to untangle

our fates: health and sickness,
bear and bull, we rise and fall together,
advance, retreat, advance.

Good times are just around the corner.
Your wit will carry you far.
And sometimes a riddle, tongue-tied,

unfinished: *Strike while the iron is.*
Which is what we've been doing tonight
naked in our bed, this twenty-fifth

year of our making—Year of the Snake,
whose strength is a gradual
gathering, a slow crawl out of the past.

Wrapped in new skin, my head
on your chest, the chopsticks
idle in the blue china bowl,

we tease out our newest fortune:
You will never have to buy
another umbrella. Meaning,

we will never lose, or be lost, again?
Or, the sun will always shine?
Or, the umbrella stashed in the back

of the closet, the one we've stood beneath
at burials, at christenings and weddings
when the weather surprised,

is shelter enough. The plain,
black umbrella with a few broken spokes,
the one we keep forgetting we have.

Out of Context

I want to be taken
like a whispered

rumor or a message
broken over water

by telegraph keys.
To be taken out

of this bed, its scrolled
masthead announcing

another decade together,
whole books written

around our words: *Do you?*
The cat. Mortgage.

Love, let's lift
the words from our tongues

before they land
in the breakfast cereal,

the sink, on the rake's
waiting handle, the pile

of rusting leaves. Take them
out, like the song says,

to the ballgame. Or scissor them
from their stories the way

kidnappers ransom
small words innocent in

and of themselves—*if   love
money   now*— spelling the end

of life as someone
once knew it. Think of the scenes

waiting to be spliced
from what's left

on the cutting-room floor,
the moments as yet

perfectly unfinished:
shadows splitting, a woman's

hand reaching, a love cry
sliced in mid-gasp.

A Definition

Love, you once told me,
means you could give your wife
an enema if it came to that.
You say the sweetest things, I thought.
I was young and childless and could not
imagine allowing anyone that much access.
When we met, you were already a father.
I married you partly for that. My mother
always said every man wants a son,
and yours was so conveniently there,
courtesy of a first wife I knew only
through the signature on the backs
of child support checks. Tonight
we talk of your mother's cancer
which once in a letter I misread as *career,*
and it might as well have been,
she gave so much to it. Now that it is done,
it is not the memory of her pain
that breaks you, but the unnatural tilt of the wig
and the sound of your old bicycle horn
which she retrieved from the attic
and carried with her to the bathroom
so your father could hear
if she got stranded, the way a wild gander
hears the distant honk of his mate
and swoops down to answer.

Last night after an expensive dinner
we made anniversary love
in a bed so crowded with years
I once told you I don't want to know

who else is in here with us,
all the lives and loves confused.
Hours later, the veal turned to poison,
sweat slid off my nakedness
as I shivered in the bathroom—
my head in the waste can—and called out,
amazed to see you suddenly there,
naked in the blue fluorescence.
And then, in some remembered gesture,
you placed a washcloth on my forehead.
When I was finally emptied, I looked up
into the mirror, saw our future,
your father hurrying through the door:
then *one of us* holding *one of us*.

GESTURE

In the days my father's mother
was dying, the room was busy
with daughters. My father brought flowers,
wrote checks, touched the face
powdered and creamed
after a morning bath.
Their shared breathing filled, emptied
the room. He stared at his hands:
what would be asked?
The Pietà teaches only
how a mother holds a *son*.
As a child too young for his father's
field, he'd followed the dark braid
coiled on his mother's head. The weight
of day loosened it; by evening, pins slid
onto the swept floor. His mother
would sigh, untie her apron
and, still as a child, allow
the undoing: the comb's ragged
teeth, sparks igniting the air,
her son's hands smoothing, smoothing.

A TELLING

Each day in first light
my mother the child

left mother and sister
and followed her father

swinging buckets toward
the hay steam of barn

where brown cows waited.
One was small enough

for her hands.
The black eyes rolled

in their sockets to greet her.
While her father soaped

udders, wiped them clean,
she balanced on a stool

and leaned into the cave
between belly and sac.

Sixty years later,
her parents long dead,

the farm gone
to seed, then auction,

she stalls at the telling.
Words, she says, can't *express*—

unaware she has given
the old farmer word

for what happens between hand
and milk. *It's all lost,*

she says. *Let me try,* I say.
It was early morning.

The straw was sweating
manure and rain.

Your father was whistling.
A tail bristled your ear.

You pulled gently,
your father nodded.

Patience, he said.
Flies made a blue buzz.

The first white stream
hit the bucket and sang.

Winter Solstice

I

In this dark season—the sun declining, the earth wearing
    herself down—the planets decide, for the first
and only time this century, to string themselves together like pearls
    on the neck of a stunning black woman, a starred
path to lead the wise and foolish to a stall on winter's edge.
    I've never seen a haloed God-child, but my youngest nephew
has ears so wondrously large, light shines through them—ears
    like leaves of new cabbages or other tender delight that feeds
on cold and dark. He was born on the first day of a January war.
    In the birthing room a television muted the rumbling
tanks filled with boys (one might have been yours) setting sail
    across an ocean of sand. *What a day to be born!*
my mother gasped. My sister gripped the rails and waited.

II

We make so much of brightness: skyscrapers, towers, a cityscape
    blazing, another kingdom crowned with stars.
Even the construction cranes, awkward birds outside my window,
    are chasing tails of light. We can't get enough—
all night diners, cable access, white dishes aimed at the heavens.
    Small star   it's no wonder
we wonder where you are.

III

Morning, but barely: a warm coffee mug, the wheeze
    of a city bus making the difficult corner, its lighted interior
filled, faces muffled in scarves and duty. Some sleep

like children—mouth open, cheek pressed against the glass.
A white truck passes, promising *Baked While You Sleep*,
  and I think of all the hands it takes to give our daily bread—
farmer, thresher, baker, trucker, shelver, checker, bagger.
  In the half dark someone is rising, steaming a uniform,
lathering a beard. A hotel attendant bears croissants
  on a silver-hooded tray, a waitress pins her thick red hair
beneath a net, a conductor leans against the whistle. Soon
  the babies will roll past in the Day Care's six-seater, a United
Nations of children pushed uphill by a panting girl
  who will relinquish them to mothers at the end of the day.

IV

An angel shattering the doorway with light,
  and Mary astonished, one arm lifted to ward off the glare:
How can this be, when I have known no man?
  Her eye sees beyond the shame, the town's veiled
whispering, beyond even the heavy waiting, *gravity, gravitas,*
  the uphill travel, the travail—to the child himself, the steamy
head against her breast. Son of woman, or God? Gold, yes,
  and frankincense. But myrrh, bitter sweet of sepulchers—
what manner of gift is this? *Fear not*, says the angel.
  A holy wing will overshadow you and the seed of light be sown.

V

Under cover of darkness: what better place to hide a king?
  Darkness our womb, our shawl, our flight to Egypt
with the doomed boy, our root cellar, storm shelter, underground
  railway, freedom tunnel, preserver of condemned things.
He will hide me, the psalmist writes, *under the shadow of his wing.*
  So the God-ghost grows feathers and swoops down,

and the Father, all windy spirit and light, plants a son in the belly
    of a woman made of blood and flesh and hair,
whose form casts a shadow. Shadows define us: earthly substance.
    Human. That's why Peter Pan came flying home for his.
Stitch it back, he cried to Wendy. *Even if it hurts.*

VI

On the sidewalk outside my window a man
    shuffles past, swaddled for all seasons. Beast of burden,
carrying his life on his back.

VII

When the moment was accomplished for my sister
    to deliver, I glanced at the muted screen where doomed boys
waved, then to the other screen—her heartbeat, the child's—
    and a head crowned the darkness and my nephew broke forth
into medical light, and they suctioned the scream
    from his mouth and glory to God in the lowest
and highest places, he was alive.

VIII

While I squalled in my mother's arms, my father was half
    a world away, flying under cover of darkness. *Black as far
as the eye could see,* he says. His night fighter swooped
    over convoys, over villages, its wings loaded with fire.
What else could we do? We had orders. He says *we*, but only *he*
    now, alone, recalls the Korean winter, the unearthly
brightness from the heavens, the moon alive on snowy fields.
    Then one wing fluttered and he was down, the open cockpit
sheathed in ice, his body numb, arms packed above his head

as if in surrender. *If I could have reached my pistol,*
he says…and turns away. Then radio static, distant
    voices stuttering his name.

IX

The long watch over, my friend buries a brother,
    another pearl in the string, another seam in the national quilt
of young men, daughters, fathers, sons. *He telleth the number*
    of the stars; he calleth them all by their names.

X

Some years the shadow spreads its wing. We hide beneath it.
    In the Christmas of the Great Family Sadness,
my mother stripped the tree, bauble by bauble, even the angel topper.
    Too much, she said, and placed a naked tree at the window.
Strange, she wrote later, *how beautiful it was.* Beautiful, too,
    this bare scene from my window. A leafless oak,
bones against a white sky. Gray doves tipping across the gravel,
    their shadows pumping before them. Beauty is a dance
of light and shade: a woman's creased eyelids, chiseled cheekbones,
    the carved space in her neck, the hollow he can't stop
kissing. Hungry landscapes, furrows, grooves, valleys, scooped out
    bowls. For God so loved the emptiness, he created it first:
earth without form, magnificently void, and darkness
    upon the face of the waters. *Deep light* is what explorers call
the glimmer from the belly of the sea. Too faint to be perceived
    by human eyes, its source unnamed, still the sea glows,
spiritual, luminescent, lit miraculously from within.

Index Of Poems

New Poems

from *Naked as Eve*

from *The Intersection of X and Y*

from *Mrs. Houdini*

from *Mother Tongue*

from *One Word Deep*

About the Book

This book is typeset in Granjon which was designed in 1928 for Linotype by George Jones. It is named after the sixteenth-century French printer, publisher, and lettercutter Robert Granjon, who is noted in particular for his beautiful italic types. A common pairing is the romans of Claude Garamond (a contemporary of Granjon's, whose roman types were of exceptional quality) and the italics of Robert Granjon.

Cover photo from *The Third I (Eye)*
Copyright © 2006 by Whirlwind Creative, Inc.
Photography by Terry Parke
Cover Design by Donald Devet
Typeset by Robert B. Cumming, Jr.

REBECCA MCCLANAHAN is a poet, essayist, fiction writer, and teacher whose literary awards include the Wood prize from *Poetry*. Her most recent book, a suite of memoir-based essays entitled *The Riddle Song and Other Rememberings*, won the 2005 Glasgow Award. She has also published four previous volumes of poetry and three books about the writing craft, including *Word Painting: A Guide to Writing More Descriptively*. McClanahan's work has appeared in *The Best American Poetry, The Best American Essays, The Kenyon Review, Georgia Review, Gettysburg Review, Boulevard*, and numerous anthologies. She has received a Pushcart Prize in fiction, a New York Foundation for the Arts Fellowship in nonfiction, a P.E.N. Syndicated Fiction Award, and (twice) the Carter prize for the essay from *Shenandoah*. McClanahan, who lives in New York City, teaches in the low-residency MFA Program at Queens University in Charlotte, the *Kenyon Review* Writing Program and the Hudson Valley Writers' Center.